VOICE FROM THE SEA

VOICE FROM THE SEA

AND OTHER REFLECTIONS ON WILDLIFE & WILDERNESS

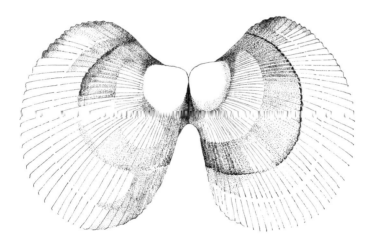

Written and Illustrated by

Margaret Wentworth Owings

Introduction by Jane Goodall

MONTEREY BAY AQUARIUM PRESS

Monterey, California

Monterey Bay Aquarium Press, Monterey, California
The mission of the Monterey Bay Aquarium is to inspire ocean conservation.
Copyright © 1998 by Monterey Bay Aquarium

The publisher gratefully acknowledges the generosity of The Bancroft Library. Many of the essays that appear in this book were adapted from Margaret Wentworth Owings, *Artist, and Wildlife and Environmental Defender*, an oral history conducted in 1986-1988 by Suzanne Riess and Ann Lage, Regional Oral History Office, The Bancroft Library, University of California, Berkeley, 1991.
[BANC MSS 92/717c]

Managing Editor and Book Editor: Nora L. Deans
Editors: Roxane Buck-Ezcurra and Christina Joie Slager
Design & production: Carole Thickstun, Ormsby & Thickstun Design
Printed on woodfree paper in Hong Kong through Global Interprint

Library of Congress Cataloguing-in-Publication Data
Owings, Margaret Wentworth, Voice from the sea: and other reflections on wildlife and wilderness /Margaret Wentworth Owings.
p. cm.
Includes index.
ISBN 1-878244-23-X
1. Zoology 2. Wilderness areas. 3. Nature conservation.
I. Title.
QL45.2.095   1998
333.95--dc21   908-31930
                    CIP
Owings, Margaret Wentworth

ISBN 1-878244-23-X

Front cover photo: Sisse Brimberg
Back cover photo: Larry Dale Gordon

THIS BOOK IS DEDICATED

TO RACHEL CARSON AND

HER INSPIRING WORDS

"We are all united in a common cause.

It is a proud cause, which we may serve

secure in the knowledge that the Earth will be

better for our efforts. It is a cause that has no end."

The closing words of Rachel Carson's acceptance speech after receiving the National Audubon Society's Gold Medal, December 3, 1966.

Along the Tenaya Road

Contents

Preface

The writings of Margaret Wentworth Owings create a rich chorus of voices from the sea, the forests, and wildlife, and give to all who read them "…a profound sense of a person who has always been hungry for the beauty of nature, language, and art."

Her treasures are her notebooks, filled with favorite lines from other authors and poets, as well as her own observations. "My notebooks are deeper than 'favorite things,'" she says. "They are things that say something to me. And beautiful things. I love the power of a beautiful expression, I love to read it, and when I find it, it gives me quiet pleasure. The choicest bits I've ever jotted down in notebooks have been what I observed as I walked along or drove along or I was on a hike and sat down on a rock and jotted down the moment, the absolute moment of hearing this birdsong, or watching an incident happen…Things like that help me. There are a lot of things in these notebooks that help me personally, and they might help other people, too."

This book includes many of her favorite pieces. Her public speeches and articles, in particular those published in her "Cliffside Seat" for Friends of the Sea Otters' newsletter column, have further inspired informed advocacy, and stewardship. They have rallied people to influence legislation, and in turn, preserved wilderness for the wildlife she cares about so passionately.

Margaret Owings did not intentionally set out to be a conservationist, but meeting Rachel Carson in the 1960s reinforced her commitment to preserving the natural world. Both women illustrate the "vital role that literature can play in interpreting the natural world, and the enduring ability of one dedicated individual to make an impact on society" as Paul Brooks writes in his preface to his book about Rachel Carson, *The House of Life.*

Margaret's indomitable will to protect endangered species has left a legacy to all generations. She founded Friends of the Sea Otter in 1968 and was the first to remove the bounty on the mountain lion. Thanks to her, we are able to see frolicking sea otters in California's coastal waters, or come upon the footprint of the cougar in its woodland habitat, or walk through the glory of the old growth redwoods.

Margaret has received many major conservation awards in this country, including the National Audubon Society's Medal, the United Nation's Environmental Program's Gold Medal Award, and the U.S. Department of the Interior's Conservation Service Award.

To know Margaret Owings is to meet elegance and strength, charm and wit, vision and conviction. Perhaps her dear friend Wallace Stegner best described her in the introduction to her oral history, *Artist, and Wildlife and Environmental Defender,* published by the Regents of the University of California in 1991:

> Margaret Owings is more than meets the eye, but what meets the eye is not merely attractive but striking. Yet under the finished surface is a woman with principles and convictions, a woman acutely sensitive to natural beauty and friendly to wild things, and committed to their rescue and preservation. In her service on the California State Park Commission, in her collaborations with her husband Nat Owings, the noted architect, in the conservation of the Big Sur coast, she has shown herself to be as intelligent and imaginative as she is stubborn. And she is scared of nobody.

A common interest in environmental issues threw the four of us together. At different times, Nat and I both served on the National Parks Advisory Board, and once we shared a three-week inspection trip to the Everglades, Puerto Rico, and the Virgin Islands. What a wonderful bundle of convictions and contradictions she is. (The contradictions are only apparent, the convictions are bedrock). She has worked her head off to save the sea otter and the mountain lion, and she has seen some success, and with luck will shortly see more. She makes herself at home in the hurly burly of controversy and contention.... Nobody can listen to Margaret Owings' account of her life without becoming acquainted with one of the most effective wildlife conservationists and one of the great spirits. We count ourselves lucky to have been with her on some of the occasions she records, and to have known Nat, who while remaining supremely themselves, made a marvelous team.

> Wallace Stegner
> May 10, 1990
> Los Altos Hills, California

This book presents a selection of Margaret's best writing, both published and unpublished, to show in her own words how she achieved what she did.

INTRODUCTION
by Jane Goodall

WHAT AN HONOR to write an introduction to a book by one of my real-life heroes. For years I have cited Margaret Owings's campaign to save the California sea otters as an example of what can be achieved through the persistence, determination, resourcefulness, and passionate conviction of a single person. If Margaret had not taken up this cause, these sea otters, these utterly engaging animals, might be extinct. Instead, thanks to Margaret and a handful of dedicated supporters, they are protected—and thriving.

It was Margaret who first introduced me to these enchanting animals. I remember it distinctly—slowly our little boat approached a mother, floating on her back in a kelp bed. We saw the bright-eyed baby on her belly, and it was like coming face-to-face with creatures crafted by Disney. And then a big male surfaced right by the boat. He had an abalone in his paws. Rolling onto his back he laid the shellfish on his chest and cracked it open with a rock that he was holding under his arm. He scrunched up the delicacy with obvious and messy enjoyment. I'd had a special fascination for tool-using behavior of his sort ever since observing the Gombe chimpanzees using, and making, tools.

Margaret had spent hours watching otters, through binoculars, from the porch and from the windows of her quite extraordinary house. "Wild Bird" is well known as an architectural wonder. Designed by Nat, her architect husband, it seems to be part and parcel of the sheer cliff to which, impossibly, it clings. Great slabs of living rock are built into the rooms; transparent floors provide views of the pounding waves far below. "It can't be done," Nat was told. That was all he needed—the house slowly took shape in obedience to his dream and his will.

The same day I was introduced to sea otters, I stayed the night at Wild Bird and watched the sun sink into the golden ocean, listened to the plaintive calls of the seabirds, the haunting barks of the seals, the ceaseless slapping and sighing of the waves breaking on the rocks below. And no sign of human development—as far as the eye could see to the north, to the south, the shore life was wild, deserted, utterly glorious. And that, I soon discovered, was another victory that could be chalked up to the tireless efforts of Margaret and Nat.

A few close friends came for dinner. Wine and conversation flowed. And the more I listened, the more my admiration for this quiet and gentle-seeming woman grew. She had accomplished so much; no issue, it seemed, was too hard for her to tackle. She took on anything that she felt really strongly about. And she would never give up.

After we had eaten, Margaret read to us some of her beautiful and poetic prose. Her vision of the wild places of the world. And though some 20 years have passed since, my memory of that evening is still vivid. Margaret's voice against the background sounds of the sea and its creatures. A precious memory.

A few months ago Margaret and I again sat together in Wild Bird. She told me of the various issues she was battling—one of which was the perennial fight to protect the mountain lion in the hills of California. She had not changed at all, I decided. We talked of so many things, and the hours flew by much too fast.

As we looked out at the incomparable view, I thought of the countless thousands of animals and plants that owed their very existence to this one woman. I thought of the many people who could gaze at the unspoiled coastline, even as I gazed then, and give thanks to the one who had fought so hard to protect it. Margaret Owings has earned her very special piece of paradise on earth.

THE DREAM

The dream turned real this morning,

as soft edges in the shimmering haze

became knife-sharp,

and beauty walked right through the open window.

THE WAVE

I watch the wave

gradually take shape,

down the long ribbon

of coastline,

under a clear dawn.

Born out of elongated shadows,

it moves toward shore.

Driven by the winds,

and that mysterious lunar power,

it meets the undertow

draws back, then arcs over it,

to explode on the shore

with a crash of white radiance!

At that moment one is reminded of the words of Gavin Maxwell:

"The morning is like the childhood of life

when the blood sings

and it is easy to laugh."

VOICE FROM THE SEA

HOME IN WILD BIRD

MAY I SPEAK OF THOSE MOMENTS after sunrise, when the mist is rising from the sea and the fog is fingering the canyons of Big Sur? Each day lies before us, guarding our lasting plans for continuity. And the sea, that life-giving support, lies quietly below us in its undisturbed immensity. At times, one hears only a broad current of sound, too subtle for human ears to define. Is it the sea otter twisting the kelp fronds to make a hammock for rafting—or perhaps the flap of cormorants' wings touching the water as they dive?

> *Again, I draw*
> *within the empty hour, riding the tides*
> *on kelp beds off a strand, catching the silent whisper*
> *of a power—*
> *as far-flung waves and lonely shores*
> *shift sand. And in clay-colored dusk*
> *when swallows power, tipping the air*
> *with burnished points of call, no sounds delineate the empty hour,*
> *no entry but the drifting rise and fall.*

Planning a dwelling in this remote spot was a new world for my husband, a new concept, a new dream for both of us, and we named it Wild Bird. Yes, my husband, Nathaniel, and I acquired this point of land in Big Sur in 1952, when roads were rough and people were few. Nathaniel Alexander Owings was a well-established architect from Cornell University who primarily focused on glass towers in the cities. But this change meant much more than turning a corner— for we sought to turn a corner of life and developed a new sensitivity among the rocks and trees of Grimes Point. We deliberately constructed a precipitous path edged with natural stone, wild sage and native grasses—leading down to the main door, entering a world of uncommon peace.

Above us, the Santa Lucia Range folded its shadows at 2,000 feet and poured its streams down the redwood canyons and dropped them into the sea.

Yes, it was a natural region where wildlife converged. Peregrines with sharp-edged cries rose from their aerie, circling the house for other life on the wing. (I once asked young ornithologists why these falcons chose our point of land for their home and was told that the narrow point of this steep silhouette reaching out into the sea was a perfect hacking site. There were 11 natural hacking sites between Morro Rock and Santa Cruz when I was told this—but today there are far fewer.)

Canyon wrens selected it as well, nesting in the cracked granite, close to the house for safety, cascading their songs like falling water. Rare ring-tailed cats, with their stunning black-and-white tails, appeared at dusk, slyly watching wood rats and chipmunks whose cheeks bulged with seeds . . . and the five young foxes who crept out of the brush for scraps of food, raised their pointed noses to the full moon and joined the ebullient call of the coyotes across the canyon.

But standing proudly alone was a presence encircling our house, a female cougar with her hoarse whisper in the canyon, or her muted voice calling her kitten to follow.

A Life More Noble

It was late one afternoon in June, 1957, when my husband and I were seated on our porch making plans for the future and watching the fog bank move in toward shore. We talked about the large, white Steller sea lion, a bull the old-timers in Big Sur had observed returning to this beach every year. That day, he loomed tall on top of the largest sea mammal rock, directly beneath our house, surrounded by five females and their young. He presided over a glorious harem, an absorbing unit of life to observe. Suddenly, three shots from a high-powered rifle shook the air; looking up to the coast road we saw a man standing there, holding a gun.

Below us, the great white Steller sea lion plunged off the rock into the sea, a cloud of red blood spreading around him as he dove and twisted, his life pouring out in the waves. His handsome white coat turned vermillion as he battled against a force he had no power to control. Within minutes, his strength was gone and he sank below the red stain on the water.

There was nothing we could do. I breathlessly ran up to the road, and as I reached our gate saw the truck pull away.

We had watched a king die.

Only one thing was left to do, and I began it immediately—a letter filled with descriptive emotion to the *Monterey County Herald*. I ended it by saying, "I was strongly moved by this incidental, needless murder, without reason, by a man who had extinguished a life quite obviously more noble than his own." The editor placed it on the front page of the *Herald*, and it was weeks before the issue died down.

Orcas and Sea Lions: Rhythmic Predation

MANY ARRESTING AND LONG-REMEMBERED INCIDENTS have been viewed from our porch. I can clearly recall them in every detail. Seated on the porch bench, I often enjoyed working on my stitchery—with a constant glance to the world below, where, in the words of Rachel Carson, "sight, scent and sound" enveloped me. Our powerful old navy telescope, attached to the porch railing, could instantly clarify the details of sea mammals moving in the waters below.

One day, seated thus, I looked down upon the sea lions (*Zalophus californianus*) and noticed about 80 of them drawn up on the stony beach, while others drifted near shore. Suddenly, I watched a tension among them, even felt it myself. Those in the water barked sharply, chuffing in alarm, while those on the beach, hearing the alarm, poured out into the water, in what we might call "an instant terror," and joined the swimmers.

At that moment, 12 orcas (*Orcinus orca*) rounded the bend of Grimes Point from the north with a steady, rhythmic pace. Swimming precisely in pairs, they moved directly toward the sea lions. The leader was a stunning matriarch, perhaps some 22 feet long, with a large bite notched out of the curve of her tall fin.

I reached for the telescope and focused upon a vivid drama. The sea lions formed a tightly rounded mass of heads, turning frightened faces toward the approaching orcas. As these huge animals reached the sea lions, their pair formation divided, encircling the frightened animals. So precise was this act, it resembled dressage at a horse show. Then, abruptly, as if a whistle had blown, the orcas arched their bodies and dove under the sea lions, which, in turn, instantly pulled their heads under water.

At this point, the surface of the water appeared calm, with no sign of the devastation occurring below. Then the orcas reappeared, cutting through the quiet surface, assuming their original formation, a number of them still devouring sea lions. The large matriarch with the notch in her fin returned to her leadership role and led the pod down the coast. Through the telescope, I could still see this amazing procession, unwavering in its alignment, over a mile away.

A strange silence prevailed below. Some of the sea lions made their way back to the beach, bleeding from deep gashes on their bodies. Others turned north without a sound, to flee from the orcas. The beach was nearly empty for a long time, littered only with the victims' bodies. Gulls gathered to peck at their remains.

THE TARGET

BELOW OUR HOUSE IN BIG SUR, the canyon drops steeply down into a region of shadowed solitude. This canyon is frequented by many animals, including a number of deer that browse the slopes and deep walls of the running stream. Although it is rarely visited by us or others, it can be viewed in part from the highway above.

One afternoon, my husband chose to walk down our canyon trail. Under the redwoods below our house a doe lay dead on the path, shot through the neck. She had obviously struggled along the trail into the shelter of the redwoods where she knelt and attempted to give birth to a fawn. The doe was a perfect specimen, and the little fawn, with its spotted coat and beautifully formed little head, was just seeing the light of day when its mother died. The harsh world of man into which this delicate fawn was born didn't give it a chance.

Why did this man with a gun shoot this superb little doe? Not for food. Not out of fear. Not even for a prize trophy. No, this man with a gun in his hand shot the deer for a target, a brief moment of satisfaction as he hit his mark. And that moment of man's satisfaction not only caused an animal agony and death but destroyed a future generation as well.

This little tragedy is a symbol of the havoc caused by the gun in hand, the thoughtless negative element cutting down a positive element of beauty, a doe in the spring giving birth to a fawn.

The interwoven pattern of wildlife in our Santa Lucia mountains is a frail web of infinite value. Without wildlife, our canyons and slopes will lose an intangible value and become empty and dead.

What are the rest of us doing while the few are out looking for a target?

WHERE THE DOE LAY

Sought the shadowed form

Of the hermit thrush

But the jay came.

Parting tall grasses for columbine,

I found iris.

Down by the stream

The song was loud at twilight

And the scent of nettle and mint

were like swift water.

Silencing the Coastal Waters

I'VE OFTEN FELT THAT IF I COULD BE BORN AGAIN, I would choose to be a sea lion. Their love of life, their ease and grace of motion, gliding in balance with the storms, floating with leisure in the swells, all in the precarious and changing world between the sea and the land. They roar and talk to one another, living in groups, yet remaining free and individual in action. These things I admire and envy, return to and learn from.

Whenever Nat and I were away as we were in April, 1960, there was a great tendency for things to crop up as soon as we were out of sight. But this one was a whopper: A small article in the newspaper (two or three inches long) announced that California's Senate Fish and Game Committee had approved a resolution to slaughter three-fourths of the 15,000 California sea lions along the coast—a death sentence from the salmon industry. The California Trollers Association proposed an "easy method—use depth bombs." Yes, depth bombs to kill every form of marine life along our coast.

Needless to say, I wept with rage and frustration. But there might be a few weeks before this resolution passed the assembly. The next morning I wrote a letter to the *Monterey County Herald*. "How can one small group of the salmon-fishing industry, order a mass killing—so merciless and self-seeking? Write today or the voices of our coastal waters will be silent."

I had no idea how to deal with the legislators in Sacramento, so I hired two attorneys as lobbyists, the Guptas. They immediately researched the diet of sea lions and found it to be primarily lamprey eels and fish of no commercial value, although sea lions did prey on salmon returning to rivers to spawn. Then we emphasized the state of the rivers in which the salmon spawned—at risk from dams and forest cutting, pollution by toxins, and thousands of fishermen crowded together with nets.

One full-moon night, I was awakened by an avalanche of sound and leapt out of bed to see men standing on the edge of the road above the sea lion beach—throwing bombs down onto the herd of sleeping animals. There was a tremendous roar from the explosions and the sea lions crying out in a death struggle.

"Shoot 'em like skunks and rats" were words used by some of the legislators. But we defeated them! I hardly dare tell you that another bill was immediately introduced, this time attempting to placate me. It read in part, "to kill all the sea lions on the coast of California except those at Point Lobos and those on the beach below the Owings' house." Needless to say, I was so shocked and insulted by this maneuver that with the continued help of the Guptas, the media and my poetry about the sea lions' glorious music and their kaleidoscope of forms, sea lions were to become known as one of California's greatest delights.

TIMES AND TIDES

A Winter Walk on Point Lobos

*"A world that keeps alive the sense of continuing creation—
a relentless drive of life . . ."*

—*Rachel Carson*

 This November afternoon, under a silver sky, I am drawn to Point Lobos State Reserve—wanting once again to awaken an attitude of mind that develops each time one ventures into this kaleidoscope of overwhelming sounds of the sea, the cadence of sea lions and the wild cry of gulls. It's an attitude of mind that grows out of the movement of tides and winds and birds on the wing and touches a nostalgia in the scent of sage and bracken and winter-dried stalks of flowering plants mixed with the smell of brine.

The attitude is further crystallized by the mysticism of the ancient Monterey cypress, reaching back to the Pleistocene epoch, still holding to the character of its early forebears, clinging to the edge of the continental shelf.

Only foresight on the part of the few kept the rarity of Point Lobos intact for public enjoyment. Its history includes 23 years of whaling, 8 years of coal mining and granite quarrying, 30 years of operating an abalone-canning factory, and the devising of a city plan to cover most of Point Lobos with a gridiron of streets for 1,000 residents.

These intrusions into what has been called "the greatest meeting of land and water in the world" ended in 1898 through the purchase of Point Lobos by A. M. Allen, a man who valued its beauty and held it without further desecration. In 1933, the state of California purchased 400 acres of Point Lobos for a state park reserve, which today has grown to 1,250 acres. In 1973, Friends of the Sea Otter joined in the effort to establish a marine ecological reserve in the waters adjoining Point Lobos. All marine life—plants and animals—is now protected within this reserve.

The sign at the entrance gate reads, "Sea Otters in Residence," and a sheet is handed to each visitor who makes an otter inquiry. It begins, "The sea otter is without doubt the most observed and beloved marine mammal of Point Lobos State Reserve." When asked how many otters are in the reserve, the answer, almost by rote, is "52 adults and 15 pups counted last summer by the ranger, with numbers fluctuating as the otters move in and out."

"How many visitors are interested in otters?" I asked, and was told, "Easily one-third of the people inquire where they can see otters." Since the visitor count was 330,000 last year, it suggests that well over 100,000 people a year register keen interest in these animals.

Leaving the gate to drive through somber tunnels of Monterey pine, one's mind suddenly shifts as one reaches the shoreline. The low tide is rising, and the water swells and slides toward the shore with a heavy cloak of kelp on its shoulders—only to break on the rocks with a white explosion.

A great blue heron, balancing itself on a canopy of kelp, catches my attention. Its bill suddenly darts down, only to snap back, clutching a silver fish, which slides down the narrow pipe of its throat. The heron resumes its former dignity.

Water is rushing into a finger cove and with it a flash of brilliant blue wing—kingfisher blue! It plunges its strong beak into the moving water, snapping up blennies, the small fish often found in tide pools.

And now an otter is emerging from under a rich pattern of kelp, shuttling its way up through the strands, clutching a purple urchin. These kelp forests are healthy islands of life, not alone for the otter's security or the heron's launching pad. They are refuges and shelters for millions of tiny animals, and they sift down nutrients to abalones, crabs and other invertebrates and fish in the sea gardens below. These sea gardens are tended by sea otters, who by removing the urchins, which feed on the holdfasts (the root structures anchoring the kelp to the rocky bottom), help to shape the ecology of the nearshore waters of Point Lobos.

Everywhere I look are interwoven strands of the pattern, some decorative, some utilitarian. Lacework, like the tiny prints of the sanderling I am now watching—quick running steps, pecking at the folds of white spindrift over sand. The prints wash away as soon as the step is taken. Everything is transient where the sea meets the shore.

The otter is transient—here and gone, then here again. I see one now somersaulting in the rolling swells; over and over it goes, washing off crumbs from its past meal. A gull waits for the salvage, and like the gull, I too wait, enjoying a sense of peace.

Out on the rocks, sea lions honk and rasp, blowing horns to the winds. Four brown pelicans flap south, probably to join that fringe of cormorants on Bird Island, a lively spot where the clatter and excitement of seabirds competes with the undertone of sea lions. As I walk south, I may find mother otters with pups rafting in sheltered coves near the island. I listen to the last songs of the day by the white-crowned sparrow and the wrentit, and spot a mother otter with a furry little parcel by her side. I stop to listen to a sound I love—the cracking of a shell on the stone anvil on an otter's chest. The light in the sky is pewter—the end of a perfect winter afternoon.

From Cliffside Seat, The Otter Raft, *Number 24, Winter 1980.*

Saving Carmel Beach

IT WAS IN 1952, when we were living in the Carmel Highlands and I drove past the San Jose Creek Beach where the monastery stands, that I was suddenly shocked to see tall, yellow machinery excavating the beach. One look and I sped to the Forge in the Forest, where the blacksmith Francis Whitaker—a man of no uncertain opinions—was pounding red-hot iron. I gave him my news. He cooled his fire and strode to his truck. "Get in," he said, and we speedily reached the beach and were striding toward these monstrosities. "What are you doing?" he shouted at the workmen, who suddenly looked very small and frightened. "A big steel company's gonna buy this beach, and we're measuring the sand." Francis turned to me and shouted to them, "Stop what you're doing—we'll buy it first." And thus, we purchased one mile of beach, including the Carmel River mouth and wetlands, for the California state parks.

Shall we measure time with the passage of tides? How many have come? And how many will come, rolling onto these shores, streaming over these rocks, rising and falling with the moon's course?

You and I, standing on this Pacific coast beach, might well feel insignificant as we pause to consider this passage of time. Rachel Carson, in her book *The Sea Around Us*, observes, "man often forgets the true nature of his planet and the long vistas of its history, in which the existence of the race of men has occupied a mere moment of time."

Yet during that brief period, man has managed to possess and destroy much of the earth's surface, including a large part of the limited line of coast lands. He rarely approaches a cove and beach, a cliff and inlet, with reverence for preservation. Instead, this comparatively rare area appears a fresh challenge to his ingenious ways.

"No scenic and recreational resource in the United States is more sorely in need of preservation," stated Newton Drury, chief of the Division of Beaches and Parks in California. "There is only so much of it, and there never will be more." California tends to neglect her responsibility to the nation, seeming to forget that her coast is the nation's coast, her beaches are not alone for the residents of her state, but for the people of Iowa and Kansas, the people of Wyoming and Arkansas, the people on the plains and in the mountains, as well as people from other lands.

Aside from the scientists' serious concern over the destruction of the balanced ecology of plant and animal life along this western edge of the continent, it seems hardly necessary to remind ourselves that the beauty alone should be cherished as a heritage for future generations. Possessed alone by the eye that sees it, whether it be today or two generations hence, it must be left in its natural state, promised an undisturbed permanence.

Instead, it is gradually being seized and shut off from the public view—the rocky cliffs blasted for roads, the sands trucked away, a restaurant perched on a ledge, a subdivision staked out over salt marshes, a "keep out" sign along the beaches, all records of blind self-seeking, with no mind to the future.

But in Carmel's dooryard, lying quietly in sun and fog, stretched a mile of beaches and rocks long taken for granted as a birthright by the children who played there, by the artists and writers stirred by its beauty, and by thousands of visitors who returned yearly because of it. Always a focus of poetic expression, this particular coastline radiates an undeniable air of enchantment. Now this, too, was jeopardized.

The river mouth, in the words of Robinson Jeffers, "where the Carmel River leans upon its sandbar in love with the waves," is the heart of the area, and from it the beaches fan north to Stewart Point and south close to the border of that rare headland, Point Lobos State Reserve, a state park jealously preserved in its natural condition by constant vigilance.

Behind the beaches, the Santa Lucia mountains quickly rise as background and drop their folds into the redwood canyons. One of these deep canyon streams flows into the sea over the San Jose Creek Beach at the southern end of the mile stretch.

All along this curve, large rolling breakers pile onto the sands with a powerful roar because of the precipitous shelving off of the land into immediate deep waters. Always within sight and sound of the waves, sand verbena and beach asters, with their pale foliage and lavender rays, bridge the line between salty sands and rocky soil.

Tide rocks and worn boulders break the regularity of the beaches and hold in their hollows and crevices the jewel-like sea gardens, those tiny balanced worlds of hermit crab and purple sea urchin. The blossom-shaped anemone, the pink abalone and the scarlet starfish cling to the rock walls, partially hidden by the sunset-colored seaweeds and presenting a dream world to the eye of the artist, to the curiosity of the child, or simply to you and me as we walk, free to explore and enjoy.

Sand dunes, dramatically cut through by the mouth of the Carmel River in the rainy season, separate the beach from the lagoon, where a fast vanishing type of habitat for land, shore and marsh birds holds the interest of ornithologists. The best-known visitors are perhaps the pelicans, flying in single file, flapping their broad wings slowly, and gliding to a splashing stop onto the waters of the marsh. Here they feed during the day, returning at night to their roost on Point Lobos, one of their northernmost nesting spots on the Pacific coast. Unless this feeding ground is preserved, it will undoubtedly be destroyed, and the ducks and loons, the grebes and rails, the rare white-tailed kite and the transient emperor goose will all simply disappear.

You and I might watch with interest what happened in Carmel when the town perceived that these beaches and the lagoon were actually endangered. "Carmel Copes with Threat of 'Improvement,'" ran the editorials in the local news. San Francisco papers smiled sympathetically at the furor. "The sinister shadow of progress falls across Carmel's southern exposure," chuckled the reporters. "They want the land so they can leave it be."

Some said acquisition of the property would be a move toward socialism, a move against free enterprise; others, to the contrary, felt the owners should donate the land as a public duty. Some believed that the natural scientists would prevent the people from using the area for recreation, while others groaned over the recreational crowds that would litter the beaches.

But a small group of Carmel people turned their backs on the idle chatter and prepared for action. They organized as the Point Lobos League and met at the Forge in the Forest, where the village smith stopped his hammering on the anvil, and mapped out a plan.

"The state is interested in those communities that show initiative in their own projects," he explained. "The county will match all public subscriptions we can raise, and the state will match the total of private and county funds."

Within a few months, the Point Lobos League had become a nonprofit corporation with an aim "to preserve natural scenic and recreational areas for the use and enjoyment of the people." Pamphlets were printed and distributed, donation boxes appeared and schoolchildren's posters filled the shop windows.

"This is a drive by the little people," whispered one ex-college president to his retired banker friend in a back row at a meeting in the grammar school. "But," he added, "they are the people who get things done. Watch them."

The Carmel Art Association and Carmel Crafts Guild immediately expressed their enthusiasm as a body by heroically donating 122 paintings, sculptures and handicrafts to a benefit that netted $3,300. The Carmel Audubon Society, with its special interest in wild bird life of the lagoon, donated $1,000 from the proceeds of its yearly lecture series. A Christmas card was designed featuring a Point Lobos cove, and this sold out immediately, with all profits going to the drive.

An "auction of surplus treasures" was dreamed up to include the housewife and the antique collector as both donor and purchaser.

"We are asking you (with a gentle curtsy)," ran the announcement, "to donate a surplus treasure, a choice object you can just (but barely) part with. All of these we shall entertainingly auction off on a gala day! And we promise dividends for your gifts, oh yes! A mile-long stretch of undisturbed beach permanently yours. A quiet lagoon filled with ducks, loons and herons, preserved as a bird sanctuary."

The result was an additional $3,000.

By this time, the campaign had spread far from town, and the Sierra Club, the Izaak Walton League and the Save-the-Redwoods League were but a few of the established organizations that offered their support.

A number of months passed, and the "little people" placed $15,000 with the state's contingency fund. To this, the county contributed $25,000 and, with the state's matching money, brought the total to $80,000.

But beaches were by no means won. Negotiations were carried on by the state with the owners. More money was needed, but the sinister shadow of progress had momentarily been checked, and in its place a different, heartwarming form of progress had been awakened. A new respect, you and I might say, for time and tides.

Adapted from "Saving Carmel Beach," National Parks Magazine, *April-June issue, 1952. Published by the National Parks Association, Washington, D.C.*

A Meaningful Sound

 Sitting here above the sea, I am often swept up by the roar of explosive power, mounting with the cadence of sea lions, the drumming elephant seals and the wild cries from the circling gulls. But at this quiet moment, when the sea lies calm, I sense only a broad current of sound—without definition—until my ears are pricked by the quick tap-tapping of a sea otter. Resting in a kelp bed of glassy fronds that encircle its small body, it cracks a clutch of mussels against a stone tool on its chest. A fragment of wind, flung up from the ocean, brings this meaningful sound to my ears.

I say "meaningful" because this sharp, brittle pounding has signaled the presence of the smallest of sea mammals along the California coast for millions of years. This is an ancient ritual, this cracking of shells to dislodge their edible occupants. And for millions of years, a population balance and abundance of both otters and their shellfish prey were maintained in a fluctuating natural equilibrium.

But that natural balance of marine life drastically changed when white men began to slaughter the otters for their fur. In 1741, the otters were first observed by Europeans on Bering's ill-fated Russian voyage. The swarming of fur hunters to collect their skins began a 170-year epoch of cruel greed. Sailing down the Alaskan coast to California, joined by American ships and Spanish galleons, they relentlessly pursued the last of the visible otters. In 1911, the International Fur Seal Treaty brought this period of decimation to a close, but by then the tap-tapping of the otters no longer rose from California's coastal bays and wave-slapped beaches.

Indeed, it was nothing short of a miracle—and a closely guarded secret shared by only a few—that a few otters had survived, hidden in kelp beds off remote and rugged shores. It was not until 1938, 60 years ago, when California's human population had shifted from native and pioneer stock to 6,056,000 people, that Howard Granville Sharpe suddenly realized that a group of sea otters was rafting together at the mouth of Bixby Canyon on the Big Sur coast. A renewed radiance of life had reappeared in our nearshore waters.

But it was not long before commercial abalone divers began to castigate these rare mammals as "destroyers" and sought measures to diminish their numbers. The otters desperately needed friends to speak on their behalf. And so, in 1968, 30 years ago, Friends of the Sea Otter was organized to stand firmly behind a sound conservation program for the southern sea otter.

I tend to think that Friends of the Sea Otter finds its symbol in the wave which lifts and falls, gathering momentum despite crosscurrents, despite human intrusions of toxic wastes and sewage poured into nearshore waters, despite oil spillage from increasing tanker traffic hugging the coast. Yes, everything is transient where the sea meets the shore.

We, in our struggle to guard the California sea otter, move toward our goal like the wave, startled by the mortalities from shootings, saddened by otter drownings in gill and trammel nets set in less than 20 fathoms of water, resentful of oil spills and plastic perils. And then come the heavy storms that threaten death unless there is human intervention and rescue.

The door is ever flung open to receive the unexpected—tides ebb and flow, mixing fact with idealism, science with emotional response. Thus, our growing knowledge engenders growing concern.

As George Schaller describes it: "We seek the moral values in what we do; an obligation to fight for preservation, to struggle to the best of our ability to assure ourselves, as well as the million private lives, a future."

On our 30th anniversary, we grapple with threats from vessel traffic, entrapment, oil spills and coastal pollution. California's human population is currently estimated at 33,252,000—that's millions of people on a collision course with 2,100 otters. We have learned that if we are to preserve a healthy population of these small animals, if the tap-tapping of the sea otter is to remain an inspiring motif along our shores, it will demand more foresight. It will require vision.

NATURE'S ELUSIVE MOMENTS

The Winter Storm of '83

ON THAT BLACK MORNING, the sea along the Monterey coast exploded in shock, and the towering surf, born on high tides, presented a somber orchestration through the depth of its tone. Making my way down our path along the cliff, I found myself leaning against a stinging wind.

Although winter along the California coast had commenced in a rough manner, with powerful gales and heavy rains, with a long surge of swells causing havoc on the shoreline, it was not until the end of February that the immensity broke through. One might say that any prolonged storm was a penetration into the unknown, but this one had a strangeness to its proportions. To the residents of Big Sur, it was a tumult, ravaging safeguards the people themselves had relied upon. Pouring down the steep slopes, it gouged the deep canyons and brought alive the placid mountains, moving them seaward in an organic manner— remolding the long-established folds of the Big Sur range. Something fundamental was occurring as the mud and rocks demolished the Coast Highway for many miles—then heavily dropped some 500 feet to the threshold of the sea.

Coastal residents who ventured out to experience the grandeur may have spotted what appeared to be a small dark log, sliding down a wave, tossed and spun, inundated and swept into apparent oblivion. After that momentary glimpse, the sea otter simply vanished.

And what of the pups? How can the mother otter continue to clutch her young or leave it to float as she dives for food? So slight in size during the first few weeks, this little puff of fur can be picked up by a wave and washed ashore or hurled against the rocks—its piercing cry lost in the din.

Normally, the nursing areas are cloaked in kelp for security, but the massive canopies have been destroyed this winter, ripped from the rocky floor with the fronds shredded and pulverized. The destruction of the kelp beds had an immediate effect on the distribution of the otters—leaving them widely scattered, further offshore or clustered in what little kelp remained.

When asked about their survival, California Fish and Game biologist Jack Ames expressed the belief that easily 50 percent of the pups were lost this winter. He remembered a Monterey beach walk in early March when he found two dead young otters with woolly coats, their bodies lying among masses of dead birds.

But Ron Jameson, U.S. Fish and Wildlife Service biologist, lifted our spirits when he reported from the Piedras Blancas marine field station that a female otter he had previously tagged had given birth to a pup in the churning waters near shore. Firmly holding her baby, she moved out into the storm, sculling through the barrier of waves breaking 30 to 40 feet high. Jameson doubted that the pair would survive—but the female's instinct clearly illustrated a technique for the survival of a species in a harsh environment. She sought to escape the turbulence by moving through it, paddling with her strong hind flippers to reach an unbroken expanse of great swells several miles from shore. Out there, she could feed the pup and spend days and nights licking and grooming it. It was not until three weeks later that Jameson saw her again, when, from the shore embankment, he looked down through the rain at the upturned face of this valiant little mother, her pup asleep on her chest. Hunger and home territory must have brought her back.

Sea lions were also driven to instinctive measures for survival. Fish and Wildlife biologist Glenn Van Blaricom watched Outer

Islet, the 110-foot-high landmark rock where waters were pounding over its crest while sea lions were climbing and clinging two-thirds of the way up its steep shielded side. At the same time, rancher Tom Tolman at Pecho Ranch reported six or seven sea lions seeking refuge in a freshwater pond on his inland property. But other marine mammals, such as elephant seal pups, suffered high mortality, unable to cope with the strength of the waves and the undertow. Pelagic birds, so closely associated with the surface of the sea, were unable to dive for food and left a tragic record of starved bodies along the sands. Brandt's cormorants could not nest on the bird rocks this year; winds were too strong for brooding and seas were too high for diving.

But a morning finally came, bright and quiet. The coast range steadied itself and the forces of the sea once again offered a gentle, unifying touch to the shore.

Ninety inches of rain had fallen.

From Cliffside Seat, The Otter Raft, *Number 29, Summer 1983, following the 1983 El Niño.*

CONDORS

I ONCE KNEW A RANCHER named Ian McMillan, whose family ranch at Shandon gave him and his brothers ample opportunity to watch the condors circling the skies over their ranch lands. Ian grew to know the condors well and became critical of the way they were being disturbed by curious people and photographers who scaled the steep rock walls trying to reach their desolate nests in the Sespe Gorge. Other ranchers poisoned dead sheep to attract coyotes—but those poisoned baits killed condors as well.

We became friends, and I appointed him to the board of the Defenders of Wildlife. He in turn stood with me in my mountain lion work—it was a rarity to find a rancher who attended hearings and wrote stirring letters on behalf of the lions.

I remember when Ian took my husband and me to a remote spot in a portion of the gorge where a hundred-foot needle of sandstone stood alone, with probably the last wild condor nest balanced on its tip. He didn't point anything out to us—just waited for us to focus our binoculars on the baby condor in the nest that had just spotted its parents. They were sailing high overhead, smoothly dropping down to circle the nest. They brought food to the eager young one, placing it into its open beak.

But the next step was even more fascinating. The parents began to teach the little condor to fly. They moved around it with outspread wings, close enough to touch its body. The little bird struggled to jump up and down, trying to raise itself to the level of its parents' wings, each feather spread apart from the other. The circling went on, up and up, higher and higher, and the baby struggled to flap its wings rapidly enough to fly. Suddenly, it looked down at its nest on the needle of rock, and we all sensed a real moment of fear, but the two parents kept close, slowly lowering it back to its nest. Relief flooded over us. And that's why Ian McMillan repeatedly said, "A caged condor is a dead condor." Probably more than any other bird on the planet, a young condor has to be trained by its parents.

Since that day, remarkable advances have been made by scientists striving to hand-raise and release condors, but those advances would not be possible without pioneers like Ian McMillan and others who struggled to preserve those magnificent birds.

The Ventana Wilderness Sanctuary is currently reintroducing young, captive-bred California condors to the wild with success, because biologists support the birds through their adolescence. Once they become adults, after six to eight years, these condors will raise their own offspring in the wild.

THE QUEST

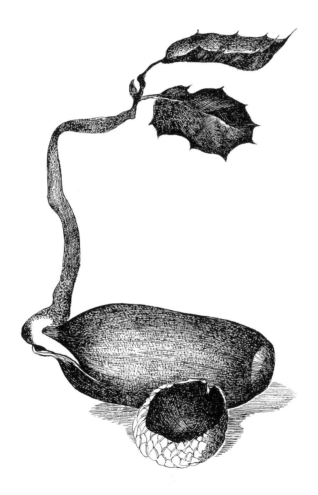

EMILY POLK

"Yet. . . is part of an eternal plan."

—*Rainer Maria Rilke*, Letters

THE PHONE RANG ONE EVENING and I heard the clear, lovely voice of a woman introduce herself as Emily Polk from Los Osos— "the valley of the grizzlies," she explained—near Morro Bay, some 75 miles south of where I live in Big Sur. I instantly learned she was hand in glove with an oak forest. Gnarled, interlaced trees with branches and evergreen leaves creating a ceiling of green atmosphere, broken only by light and shadow, and trunks that stretched out like park benches only a foot from the ground. Ben Polk, Emily's architect husband, described the forest: "Some of the trees are like fire, some are like ice, and some like water or wind."

The year was 1966. And I myself was consumed by park and wildlife issues, and redwood forests to the north. "It's about saving oaks," Emily said, and her poetic words describing these trees carried a quality I could not possibly resist. There was a perilous threat! A mobile home developer had just put up a "FOR SALE FOR FURTHER DEVELOPMENT" sign. Emily had already telephoned the number listed and was told quite bluntly, "You're too late! We already have a bid. But I'm leaving today for a two-week vacation and I told this fellow I'd let him know the day I return." He hesitated for a moment and added, "If you can raise $160,000 in two weeks, you can have it for a park."

Need I say, that was the moment she telephoned me to find out how she could make it into a park? I laughed a bit and asked, "Within two weeks?" I had served on the state park commission since 1963 and had been long acquainted with the patience required when dealing step-by-step with a bureaucracy for approval—not to mention the issue of finances.

"Do you have these funds?" I asked hopefully. The answer was simple: she must find a loan at least to cover this until she could get the approval of the state parks commission. Emily had already made up her mind, and she was about to have 1,000 copies made of 8 x 10 photographs of the oaks to send out for publicity. I mentioned a number of the key conservation organizations here in California, but she didn't know who they were, clarifying a fact that I hadn't yet grasped—she and her husband had just returned to California after 12 years in India. I gave her the phone number of the state park headquarters in Sacramento and suggested she phone for an appointment with director William P. Mott and his deputy, Jim Tryner. "Take with you not only the photographs but the age and history of these oaks." I said that this meant that within the next few days she had to bring geologists, biologists and anthropologists to the oak grove, for she must be ready to report these facts to the state parks commission.

She was to discover that the blackened stone fire-rings, with mounds of clamshells near at hand, were left by the Chumash Indians; that the trees were from 400 to 600 years old; that this was the last truly primitive oak forest ungrazed by domestic animals; that the weblike gray film on the trees was from two rare parasitic plants, plus early lichens in many colors that enriched the forest. A geologist explained that it took 60,000 years for the coastal land to rise from sand to become stable soil for the growth of trees, and that these ancient trees were heirs to the first seedlings. Emily had a rich story to tell the state.

The urgency increased as the days slipped by. I suggested Emily phone some friends of mine, Justin Dart and his wife, Jane. I gave them a quick call in advance, but her voice and descriptions instantly caught the interest of both of them. On her drive up to Sacramento for her appointments, she stopped and phoned Jane in Beverly Hills, who told her that Justin had agreed to make the much needed loan without interest and was sending a lawyer up to see the place and study the land maps. In the meantime, I was able to help her structure an organization of conservation-minded people for this unique new park. One of the first notes I received from her read:

> For a moment, most days, I step out on my little, brown paper launching pad you built for me, and fly off to explore the mysteries you've charted. As with most, the first glance reveals the form of the secret, but the deeper the probe, the more complex the revelation. Thank you for these adventures.
>
> Emily

I sent her up to Ansel Adams, who was enchanted by her, but when he asked if she had an acronym to shorten the title she had given these 30 acres, Small Wilderness Areas Preserved, her answer was "SWAP." Ansel laughed and asked if "small whims and purchases" might be more appropriate. Emily didn't laugh.

Dr. Edgar Wayburn, president of the Sierra Club, questioned whether the state park system could accept a new park so small in size. Pearl Chase from Santa Barbara, who had filled that lovely city with tiny parks, nodded her head in approval. Sylvia McLaughlin, wife of the president of the University of California and leader of the San Francisco Bay shoreline preservation movement, was intrigued. "A small park with a big purpose," she said.

The follow-up responses took shape in quick order. Park director Bill Mott came down with Jim Tryner and the state park commission for their first visit. Emily served them martinis and crackers on the tree trunks that stretched out parallel with the earth. Everyone was ecstatic! They were able to add Federal Park Land Funds to increase the size to 65 acres.

Justin Dart sat up in bed one morning, saying, "I think I'll do it." What will you do, asked his wife. "Give it to this oak park, not loan it to them."

Emily was to write out some magic lines to thank donors for funds. "A gift of nature is a growing gift of gratitude for the living earth renewed by hour, day, year and century. A gift of nature is an imperishable gift, never broken, torn, lost or worn, the gift that's given forever; that given once exuberantly gives itself in return, not alone to the giver or the receiver but to all creatures of Earth for all time."

I drove down and met Emily among the oaks, now a state oak reserve. She had achieved what she'd set out to do. We began to climb one of the oldest trees, climbing as high as we could. The shadow of a large horned owl gliding across the dried leaves alerted us to his presence, while we in turn drank a small bottle of champagne and gloried in that silence, a new beginning beckoning.

Emily would go on to establish a dozen more SWAP chapters in California, saving small parcels of rare quality for posterity.

Eloquent Flight of Inquiry— Rachel Carson

My life was completely changed, at a time when illness and deep concerns sent me to my bed. A dear friend brought Rachel Carson's *The Sea Around Us*, and read those stirring words aloud to me for several days. "This particular instant of time, that is mine" wrote Rachel Carson, and I was struck by the depth of that simple thought. Later, I stood on my porch savoring the immensity of its great view before me as the sight, sound and diversity stretched out in all its splendor—and I become part of it.

I had the privilege of meeting Rachel Carson at a National Audubon Award dinner where Rachel received a medal for her book, *Silent Spring*. After a magnificent brief speech, she left the room and seated herself apart from the others. I joined her, dropping down beside her chair. I wanted to tell her about the imprint she had made on my life. She listened and thanked me for telling her. Then we moved on to *Silent Spring*, her eloquent alarm about the poisoning of the environment. She said, with a wistful note in her voice, and a far-away look in her eyes," You know, I did not want to involve myself so deeply about conflict and poisons, I wanted to write about the mysteries along our shores."

As she spoke, I remembered that Einstein had once said, "the most beautiful thing we can experience is the mysterious source of all true art and science." And then I remembered Carson's own opinion, "In order to achieve, one must dream greatly, one must not be afraid to think large thoughts."

Before our meeting, I wrote her a note asking if she would care to join my mountain lion committee and help me with a letter to the chairman of the Assembly Resource Committee, Pauline Davis. Davis fancied deer and thought of lions as devious predators. Rachel wrote a powerful letter:

> I condemn bounties as unscientific and as fostering a cruelty and callousness that humanity could well leave behind in the Dark Ages. Modern studies have demonstrated the biological folly of predator control campaigns, which almost always lead to unlooked for side effects. The bounty system encourages the wanton killing of these magnificent creatures such as the mountain lion, which, besides their aesthetic value, have a useful role in nature. Until we can learn to appreciate the varied life with which we share the earth, we shall not be truly human.

I drove up to the hearing in Sacramento and watched Pauline Davis up at the podium, looking over her mail. It was a close vote, but it was her voice that won the bounty removal. I hurried down to thank her and she held up Rachel's letter and said it was a privilege to receive it!

During those precious moments I spent with Rachel, I shared an intuitive understanding of what she was physically going through from the pain of cancer. I didn't speak of it, but she said to me, "You know, I don't know who is going to carry on my work against carcinoma when I am unable to handle it." I looked into her quiet eyes and there was only one answer to tell her, that I would do everything I possibly could to see that her work would be continued. When we parted, I felt a warm bond with her and regretted that we had not become friends much, much earlier.

After her death in 1964, I immediately put together a small printed book called *A Quest* and used two hawk wings I had drawn as a symbol of victory. Below the title I printed, "Her Eloquent Flight of Inquiry." The small book raised funds to further Rachel's efforts.

An environmental organization, not yet formed, took shape under the National Audubon Society and was guided by Roland Clement and a team of scientists, lawyers, public relations leaders, and strengthened by a board of trustees on which I served for a number of years. It was named the Environmental Defense Fund and has been active from that day to this across the country and in both the sky and the sea.

The last words by Rachel at that National Audubon dinner defined a directive for the Environmental Defense Fund. They have spread across the nation—and continue to gain momentum.

"And so the effort must and shall go on, though the task will never be ended, we must engage in it with patience that refuses to be turned aside, with determination to overcome obstacles, and with pride that it is our privilege to contribute."

Jane Goodall

A PLEASURE IS FULL GROWN ONLY WHEN it is remembered. And remembering Jane's words is a vivid portion of the pleasure. She shares her own memories so personally and so generously that those of us who have heard them over the years are like a field of wildflowers suddenly blooming when the sun reaches us again.

As she so often says, words that have become etched in my mind:

> Only if we understand can we care;
> Only if we care will we help;
> Only if we help shall all be saved.

Jane has had to swim upstream often, battling against the current, but she has also known many periods of quiet listening, while learning to recognize the network of communication between the chimpanzees at the Gombe Stream Research Center in Tanzania.

Jane was particularly fascinated by the tool-using activities of her chimps. She often watched them delicately insert a long piece of grass, or a twig stripped of leaves, into tunnels in termite mounds, then pick off the crunchy termites.

Jane and her former husband, Hugo van Lawick, a splendid wildlife photographer, came to Big Sur for a visit with us and the sea otters that share our shores. She had come all this distance to watch another tool-using mammal, the sea otter, position a stone placed on its chest to crack a mollusc or use another stone as a hammer to remove the meat from a crustacean.

We took Jane and Hugo up to Monterey Bay and climbed into a small boat. As we set out in the harbor, Jane was dazzled by the fluid grace of the otters moving in their skins, their abrupt somersaults and the mothers embracing their pups.

But when our boat passed the Coast Guard breakwater, she was horrified to observe a large sea lion holding its head high but with a plastic ring from one of those discarded bottle containers tightly choking its throat. She firmly asked for the boat to stop so she could climb out onto the big rock and somehow cut the plastic band to save the sea lion's life. But we had no tool for this, and, sadly, it was a tragedy we had to leave behind. Jane remained silent on the way back.

It was many years later, in 1996, that Jane discovered baboons at Gombe, caught in snares of tight nylon cord that had become imbedded in the wrists of their front paws. Refugees from neighboring countries had come to the shores of Gombe to catch bushbucks for food, trapping the baboons by accident. Jane jumped into action, gathering two vets from Austria to fly through violent weather to Tanzania. The team darted the baboons with sedatives and removed the tightened snares. I wondered, when I read this account, if she had not had a flashback to the noble sea lion in Monterey Bay, choking to death from the plastic ring around its throat.

But that day in Monterey, we returned home to Big Sur, where friends joined us for dinner and to share the excitement and tragedies in Jane and Hugo's new film, *Wild Dogs*. We watched the film on a large screen set on a hunk of rock beside our burning fireplace. As we watched, they commented on the individual animals they had named and knew so well. The scenes of the unwanted female, cowering with her pup and tormented by the pack, were hard for all of us to bear.

Their son, Grub, was born in the wild. While still tiny, he was able to imitate the sounds of wildebeests and hyenas and other wild animals, even before he could talk.

Thinking of the rich wildlife they lived among brings back my own vivid memories of Africa. Nat and I once camped in the Ngorongoro Crater for a number of days, and walked alone at dusk to the edge of some wetlands, only to find ourselves suddenly surrounded by a clan of 10 to 12 hyenas, paying magnetic attention to us and circling closer and closer. From a distance, our guide had spotted us, and cupping his hands around his mouth, he shouted "Don't run!" I wondered uneasily if these animals might not be part of the "Scratching Rock Clan" in which Jane might well have singled out "Bloody Mary," the dominant female, to lead the way. We might call it an intangible evocation.

In turn, Jane and Hugo, during their stay with us in Big Sur, became sensitized to the barking of our sea lions, the hollow poundings of the elephant seals, the tapping of the sea otters with their stone tools, and screams of the peregrine falcons as the red-tailed hawk circled too close to their aerie.

Jane and I had ample opportunity to talk about her chimps, including Flo, mother of many, whom Jane loved. She wrote me a letter soon after their return to Gombe about Flo's death. Flo's juvenile son, Flint, fell into a deep depression. He refused to eat, was not interested in social interaction and he became sick. He built a rough nest of small branches by the stream where her body lay. He was dead within a month of losing his mother. For Jane, this was heartbreaking.

Yes, there have been many heartbreaks over the years: the polio epidemic, the males attacking their old friends who had moved south. Why did this happen? Is it a chapter in evolutionary development that leads to crowded cities and gangs of young people, whose attitudes reflect lost love, lack of caring and failure to love lives beyond their own?

Always, Jane sought knowledge and knew she had to be wiser in the ways of man. She left Tanzania and traveled around the world, concluding that she must visit the prison camps of the Holocaust to see for herself the worst evidence of human behavior. She saw ugly remnants of concrete once housing dying Jews, but there she also saw the roots and shoots of plants growing out of cracks in the concrete. These became the symbol for her program Roots & Shoots. This program is for all children, from kindergarten through universities, including children from inner cities, in need of new attitudes, in need of a simpatico exchange like the chimps who moved about the forest, caring for one another, carrying one another, caring for family members, even adopting motherless orphans. The goal of Roots & Shoots is to plant the seeds for a new environmental ethic. The program provides interdisciplinary educational materials to schools and community groups and focuses on hands-on learning, global networking and constructive action.

Jane told me about the thousands of letters she received after one of her television programs aired. In that program she met and communicated with chimps and then talked to her Roots & Shoots friends, urging them to stay together and to care for one another, and to love and care for animals.

"Margaret," she said to me, "it's magic, it's really reaching the spirits of these troubled young people with magic."

And it is your skill and wisdom, dear Jane, that will keep the miracle alive.

The Vermilion Flycatcher,
Roland Clement

We became alert the minute Roland Clement arrived at our door here in Big Sur. I had been associated with him through the National Audubon Society at the time of Rachel Carson's work on *Silent Spring*.

As Roland came through the front door, a hummingbird darted over his shoulder into the living room and up to the skylights overhead. I instantly hurried away for my bamboo pole, to which I had attached a portion of my wedding veil. (Roland expressed no surprise at this.) With a steady hand, quiet and gentle, he twisted the netting around the hummingbird and carried it out the open door to the porch. After he unraveled it, I touched a drop of honey on my finger to its thirsty tongue. Opening its eyes, the hummingbird straightened up—and vanished.

My husband and I had a picnic lunch ready, and off we went to climb the edge of Grimes Canyon, up through the redwoods and oaks. Roland was the first to point out a golden eagle coasting slowly over the tops of manzanitas, where six does were browsing. Like Roland, they were alerted to the bird's presence by the shadow of its long wingspan and dashed off into the underbrush, leaving behind a trembling newborn fawn. My husband, always a man of action, waved his arms and started to shout loudly, trying to save it from the eagle. But Roland silently touched his arm and said, "Leave it to the does, Nat. They'll save it." And this they did, nudging its head and weak legs, moving on both sides of it and disappearing into the thicket.

Adapted from an introduction of Roland Clement at the National Audubon meeting at Asilomar, California

THROUGH HIS FORESIGHT AND AWARENESS Roland Clement has developed an ethic. An ethic based on factual information which man must have to arrive at rational judgment.

During the three-and-a-half years Roland spent in Canadian Labrador with the U.S. Air Force Weather Service, his personal interest in the ecology of the subarctic took shape.

Later, with a degree in botany and geology, and a master's degree in wildlife conservation, he began to put the pieces together into the full picture of life's environment.

And so, Roland Clement has taken on a leadership role—broad, in the immensity of its view—and detailed to record the death of a robin or the sterile egg of an eagle.

For the advent of pesticides is a form of science exploited by technology
—despite the dire warnings in *Silent Spring*
—despite the barometer loss of bird life
—despite minute quantities of these chemicals now found in mother's milk
For the "last end of every maker is himself."

During the past few years, Roland Clement has worked without respite to present the pubic the knowledge that the use of hard pesticides can be destructive to our world in the far-reaching manner of the bomb at Hiroshimaóa power without human understanding!

Mr. Clement has been connected with the National Audubon Society since 1950 and has edited several volumes including *A Gathering of Shore Birds* and *Life Histories of North American Birds*.

But my husband and I associate him primarily with the vermilion flycatcher, which he pointed out to us in Arizona at the National Audubon Conference some years ago. On the slopes of Big Sur (where we live) among the towhees, the juncos, the wrentits, the jays and the quail we often long for that flash of brilliant light—a flash to follow with the eye and mind. I give you one tonight—Roland Clement.

WEAVING A STRONG THREAD

Adapted from commencement address at Bradford College, Bradford, Massachusetts, June 1, 1975.

STANDING HERE TODAY, I want first to reawaken in memory the presence of a Bradford woman, Jean Pond, whom I am proud to claim as my great-aunt. She graduated from Bradford in 1885 and returned to what was clearly her intended place in 1902 to teach the love of learning through English and other subjects for over half a century.

It was because of Aunt Jean that I came to Bradford over 40 years ago, and I return today as a further link with those of like heart and mind. I return with a warm sense of nostalgia and a hope that a strong thread will weave us together. If my message falls outside your reflections, then consider my thoughts merely random seeds of persuasion.

One of my favorite authors, Freya Stark, once wrote, "The true secret of persuasiveness is that it never converts. It speaks to its own only, and discovers to them the unexpected secrets of their hearts."

This is the day of the forward thrust and perhaps a sudden pull—and I ask a jolting question. Are you graduating into a liberated society—or are you emerging into a compartmentalized world with a repeating pattern of mediocrity or conformity? In this year, 1975, can you hold to a quality that is you? People power—3.5 billion today and 5.8 billion people in the year 2,000. A brighter, louder, and more disastrous world than anyone has faced before.

Certainly, in this brighter, louder world there are many achievements ahead which some men label as "accelerated changes" and others as "great upheavals." Many of these changes are called "progress," yet the simple faith in progress, observed by Norbert Weiner, "is not a conviction belonging to strength, but one belonging to acquiescence—and hence weakness."

But my thoughts today deal less with the progress of technology and more with progress of attitudes and insights. I am thinking of each of you, the individual, leading a privileged life with a sense of wholeness and fulfillment.

What, we might ask, are the attributes of this individual mind? The door flung wide to receive the unexpected? The wonder of miracles, the oscillations of tides, the migrations of birds, the songs of the whale—in short, the great rhythms of our planet—never fully understood?

And what might accompany this sense of wonder? Could it be faith? Faith, not necessarily in religious dogma, but faith as a way of life. For faith is always the beginning of action. As Laurens Van der Post wrote, "Faith creates; all else destroys."

> It is the not yet in the now,
> The taste of fruit that does not yet exist,
> Hanging the blossom on the bough.

And isn't freedom an attribute of this individual mind? Free to choose—free to move. To be free like a racing stream pouring over granite. But hasn't discipline carved the very channels of this mountain stream with its power-push and gravity-pull? Surely there are many times when detainment only accelerates freedom. In like manner, Marcel Proust referred to the "tyranny of rhyme" as a refinement which forces our greatest poets into the discovery of their finest lines. Yes, the creative impulse has rarely emerged from thin air.

52

The Frenchman Jules-Henri Poincaré remarked, "To invent, one must think off the point," which could mean that "the point" is the disciplined structure from which you liberate your invention.

Another attribute that you as the individual might seek could be escape. Shake the bars of your cage and emerge. Motion is often the outlet from everyday life. It can be an escape from frustrations or barriers. But can it be? This kind of escape can carry its troubles with it, and one cannot find renewal.

Rather than motion through space, a sense of place may answer much within oneself. One may find it in wilderness, an immensity, the grand proportion, the horizon against the outline of a dark mountain range. And in this immensity, one can find peace and sanity and life in the intimate interrelations of this uninterrupted wildness.

One escapes confinement in the unexplored landscape—and one can experience a penetrating moment of insight. Even a reckless moment! One can stand outside oneself in a form of satori, and the world rises before one's eyes and one sees it in all its splendor. The moment has been called "oceanic" or "cosmic consciousness."

Lois Crisler lived in the immensity of the tundra with wolves and caribou and tries to describe this experience in her book *Arctic Wild*:

> I longed for words of heightened awareness to help me feel the invisible dimension of our experience. Nothing I knew, neither music nor poetry, had the right flavor or smell. I wanted wild glory, some strange strain never yet heard.

Now, permanence does not exist here, for wilderness is alive because of change, change as a replenishing process. My husband and I witnessed this process in the moist, slender valleys of Mount Olympus in the Pacific Northwest. Sitka spruce, hemlock, Douglas-fir, and red cedar reach up like living monuments to a ceiling over 200 feet high. And one momentous day, a giant comes crashing down and stretches out horizontally, and young seedlings take root in the mosses on the fallen trunk.

But in the cathedral quiet of this forest, we began to hear the screaming of the mechanical saw on adjacent national forest lands. Thus, with the acceleration of clear-cutting on these publicly owned lands, a form of immortality and continuity are wantonly being destroyed. And as with the dense rain forests of the Amazon, threatened by development, we will loose some of the earth's supply of life-sustaining oxygen.

Yes, it will soon rest with your generation to shoulder the obligation to guard rare regions such as this, the magic regions of our country that are yours. You are free to experience them, free to return to them and free to defend them.

Sigurd Olson, the naturalist writer and philosopher of the Great Lakes region—a land of moose, wolf, beaver, bear and fox—has spoken many times of the need for animal oneness with the earth. He has spoken of the sense of close relationships—of belonging. In this age of people-power and human predation, how can one recapture this relationship? What kind of a ceremony can lead us back?

Somehow, in developing the intellect, the human mammal has pushed aside instinct and intuition. Is it our intellect that has made us the most destructive creatures on earth? Surely, not our instinct.

But as the splendor of the panorama of earth is destroyed and its interrelated wildlife disappears, this boastful intellect itself will be eroded. The loss of the aesthetic alone will perturb your psychology, your hopes, your dreams. Savage or beautiful, the written word, the painted canvas, the song that is sung—each derives its inspiration from the earth itself. In the book *Serengeti Shall Not Die* by Bernhard Grzimek, I read these simple words: "The lion walks in the red dawn and roars." A simple line of massive strength and beauty carries an impact to the nerve, the eye, the ear and the mind. The more our lives grow more artificial and more complex, the more we need to turn to things of the earth. To species other than ourselves. But when the lion no longer roars in the red dawn, the reality of this animal will disappear and the dream and precious knowledge will lose its meaning.

How many warnings do we need?

And as the last twig snaps—as wild animals disappear—what are we doing about ourselves and our own habitat? How are we going to save ourselves from ourselves?

Planned parenthood, certainly, yes, but in addition, how are we going to rein in the exploitation and its plunder by 3.5 billion people today? How?

This is where the intellect, which we realize can be a destructive force, must recognize when the fundamental elements are out of balance. We need big thinking and views broader than any yet realized. Very soon, man will no longer be able to adapt to his environment by simply changing it.

Many of your generation are involved in a new ethic—a conservation ethic. The Sierra Club is such an organization—a whiplash against the inroads on the natural environment. Here we find the idealist, the dedicated, the stubborn, the unreasonable, the spear point and the flame. Out of the flatness and conformity of a compartmentalized world, their peaks stand high.

The Environmental Defense Fund is another strong group, which grew out of Rachel Carson's cry of anguish at the poisoning of our planet. Its workers are made up of lawyers, scientists and conservation-minded citizens using the courts or legislative hearings as a theater to defeat or defend the round of issues continually before us.

The National Audubon Society, Defenders of Wildlife, Wilderness Society and Save-the-Redwoods League are a few of the outstanding established organizations backed by private funds and run by a growing breed of young people trained in the environmental fields. Certainly, the continuance of wilderness and wildlife rests upon man's cultural development, but more precisely, with those, such as yourselves, graduating from college today.

Although I work with all of these organizations, I have primarily concentrated on the California sea otter, a small marine mammal which barely survived a monstrous past at the time of the fur trade. The more I concentrated on this appealing animal, the more his true role in the structuring of nearshore communities began to unfold, and the more clearly we realized the ecological balance that existed between abalone, kelp, urchin and otter. So tightly knit is this evolutionary development that the sea otter is found to be essential to the integrity and stability of the ecosystem. Yet the southern sea otter's return was defined by many not as a rarity back from near extinction, but as a predator in competition with man.

This is the point where I came in, for it was clear that the sea otter needed a friend. Friends of the Sea Otter was formed in 1968 and today has over 4,000 members. We play a guardianship role, for these stoic little mammals are under a barrage from abalone fishermen and clam diggers who shoot, net or lacerate them with propellers even though they are on the protected list of rare sea mammals. In addition, calculated risks of oil spills from increasing tanker traffic and growing toxic wastes draining into the sea could quite abruptly threaten their existence.

What can we learn from the sea otter's survival amid overwhelming forces—a delicate life more fragile than our own? Why can't we survive the impact, as the otters did, through the ever-changing phases of our lives? Is there a way back?

To find a sense of wholeness and fulfillment, it may be necessary to turn back and descend the rungs and, in the words of Gavin Maxwell, "stand again amid the creatures of the earth and share, to some extent, their vision of it."

THE UNEXPLORED
LANDSCAPES

Moments of Wilderness

How do we define wilderness?

What is its significance? Is it an island, a region of depth, breadth and mystery, perhaps an escape for the puma in our western states or the colobus monkey swinging from a windblown limb in a forest in Africa—or is it a special place for man's spiritual needs?

A Moment in East Africa

I once had the feverish sensation of being lost in a forbidding wilderness forest which stood like solid ramparts of protection in Shimba Hills along the coast of East Africa, where cruel sailing vessels dropped anchor to capture the natives for slavery. In that region, the natives had one lodestar into which they escaped, a relic virgin forest, hundreds of feet in height, trees extinct elsewhere, with great roots entwined and no paths to mark an entrance. It was here that I followed my long-striding, well-booted British guide, Eric, as he pointed out a centipede, told me to dodge a mamba encircling a limb dipping toward us, turned his head at the cry of a turaco above us and studied the mud in which the fresh print of a Cape buffalo was gathering water. But quite suddenly, my guide was gone, and I called, "Eric!" but no sound came out of the deep forest. Baboons began to scream either at me or a nearby leopard. I called again, louder and louder, but the forest stood heavily around me in the darkness.

I was lost—but seeing a spot of light far ahead, I hurried toward it, somehow thinking to find Eric there. It was a mammoth para-macrolobium tree, fallen, breaking open the foliage ceiling for the sun to shine through. I climbed its elevated roots and held tight as my heart doubled its beat. Twenty minutes later, Eric appeared, looking for me. How could I sense fear when the natives came here to escape—and hold onto their freedom?

A Moment in New Mexico

At Canyon de Chelly, a form of wilderness overtakes one, walking alone, the size of a small grain of sand, with the magnitude of red rock walls on either side where only the shadows shift as the hours pass. Not a soul in sight but the toeholds climbing up the rock face to lifeless cliff dwellings of the past.

Now we turn to the Pecos Wilderness, in the Santa Fe National Forest in New Mexico, some 200 square miles of earth formations, canyons and granite rock promontories on which bighorn sheep climb and browse. Black bear and bobcats frequent the Douglas-fir forests, and the puma stretches out on a shelf of shadow after rubbing his shoulders over the juniper trunk. A diversity of wildlife enriches this region, but the many roads and trails draw an increasing intrusion of man.

A Moment in Big Sur

From the promontories, I return to our home on a point of land, 600 feet above the surf and rocks of the Pacific. It is the Big Sur coast, where years of citizen action have rescued much of its natural beauty and where the few residential and commercial additions have tried to conform with the character of the region. Behind us, steep slopes of redwood canyons reach up toward the ridge of the Santa Lucia mountains, where the Ventana Wilderness Area covers 167,323 acres. It is a joy to look up the steep, sun-bleached slopes spiked with yucca and swept with blue lupine in the spring!

Nerve Song of Africa, 1965

One golden twilight along the shores of Lake Manyara in Tanzania, a single male impala, moving with shoulder grace and dignity, led before us in lineal silhouette a procession of 103 females, each a live nerve, sensitive to every interplay, whisking like leaves in a hurricane or standing motionless like tall grasses on a windless day.

An intricate rhythm, not instantly comprehended, touches all wildlife in Africa—a harmony, but without a guarantee. We witnessed, again and again, the formation of order, the interjection of uncertainty and fear, the clash, the climax, the return to order—a sheet of music.

For these impala were harnessed to an order—a pattern long established—and the lone male, with stately leadership, controlled like a maestro his orchestra, in which small confusions were but elaborations of the great design.

He reprimanded the sprightly does as they leapt over one another with apparent abandon; he reestablished direction when the line abruptly reversed itself; he fought off and ejected five young bucks loitering at the rear—and, coursing the total line, he regained his lead position and drew out the music as the procession moved forward.

"What a triumph!" we exclaimed as we watched the upswept horns direct the thwarted young bucks' withdrawal.

"Oh, but he drew the short straw," came the dry retort from our British guide—a bachelor.

As dusk fell along the Mara, great herds of zebras were barking upriver. Earlier, we had watched them dancing like ice skaters, swinging the curves in pairs, racing and turning in unison—a glorious rhythm across the plains. Now, a sense of pandemonium reached us. Our guide was pleased. "Lots of lions," he said.

It is like a scent gradually growing evasive, a voice becoming silent—the sound and smell of this experience. Even now, I cannot quite recall the sense of cold fear I knew.

And now, as I commence to write, we are seated on a great fallen tree with its bleached, sun-baked elbows resting in the sandy mud of the Waso Nyiro River in the Samburu. Its dry roots fan the air—an acrobatic invitation to a family of tiny vervet monkeys.

From this centering line of observation we are becoming a part of the surface of silence, this padded, motionless hour, awaiting the imprint of sound. A scent of musk is heavy in the air—a warm smell stirring a small intuitive response, long forgotten.

"When the air has this taste of time," wrote Archibald MacLeish, "the frontiers are not far from us."

But I should write about the simplicity of this hour in another language—a language in which the rhythm is the pounding of my heart. For, this breathless August, four of us have been camping with a guide in East Africa, moving about amid wildlife—observing, not hunting—awaiting, on guard, the unexpected.

This shallow, khaki-colored river, gliding through the late afternoon, is the life vein of the Samburu. It is a habitat for crocodiles—passing through the subtleties of a parched land of wild olive and flat-topped thorn, of rock and termite mound, over which floating clouds cast oblong shadows.

But a curtain drops when one steps into the narrow riverside jungle—an abrupt plunge into another world, a world filled with secrets. Imperceptible sounds instantly become extrasensory. There is a brightness and darkness to their cadence. One feels it as well as hears it.

The slow-moving water flows not past, but through us, as the duom palms upstream are faintly rustling cool. A great worm funnel of an animal crossing cuts the bank and enters the river opposite our perch. Gardenia trees, pruned to topiary by the ungulates, stand in overgrown gardens of shrub. A giant podocarpus tree looks in DeGaulle grandeur across the river. A tiny malachite kingfisher has just alighted on a dipping twig.

Two bushbucks have emerged to pick their gentle way through the playing vervets. They nuzzle the green browse and slowly enter the water—a sense of venturing with every step. Unaware of us, they choose an oblique angle in our direction; their ears flicking flies, they disappear into the foliage, pick up an animal trail passing near the roots of our tree.

Game trails over the plains or converging on a water hole illustrate decisions made by the moving herds. This path or that path? A luxury of alternatives—but the decision and timing are fate. Each day and night, each hour of the day and night, death is waiting—death is near. Here, the animal intuition makes the selection, losing its individual sensitivity only when a herd stampedes.

Out on the rolling plains, when the slant of morning made the spiderwebs glisten in the whistling thorn, and Thomson's gazelles, with white petal ears, stood in thin, tall, pink grass against a rising sun, we have watched wildebeests bucking and racing like morning traffic down a freeway, a great reservoir of life pouring from an unknown source. Kicking their heels, ducking their heads, they jounce and pound, a soft steady thunder on the earth—an army moving and halting when fear pulsed through the column, turning back, hesitating, deciding, returning.

One can watch fear race down the line like a reverberation rolling across the land. And down by the water hole, we were suddenly to detect the rising ears of a lioness reclining on the hummock of a termite mound, two cubs at her side. She appeared heavy with meat from the night's kill, her chest and forepaws smeared with mud. Flies had settled on the blood at her jaws. Satiated, she watched the herds with indifference. As we approached in our Land Rover, her tail straightened and rose in the air. She growled. We reversed gears and withdrew.

Walking along the dust trail to this spot on the river, we too sense the tensions of decision. The destination, no matter how near, is veiled in a shadow of the unknown. Yet I am losing some of the sharp line, the delicate razor-edge of fear. Perhaps I had honed it too keen the night the elephants screamed and crashed into our camp clearing—and now, having blunted it a little, though I have lost something, I have gained more peace—an acquiescence, an acceptance.

What do I accept?

The unknown? No, never.

The mystery without deciphering it? Perhaps.

Fate? Not yet.

The inability to control my environment? Yes.

Our guide carries a loaded rifle which is never fired. He walks slowly and alertly with a moccasin tread along the game trails. His head turns constantly, his ears stretch forward like radar instruments heeding and responding to any dry crackle. I watch them move as I walk behind him. He thinks of caution as survival. Caution is a positive element relating to the intuitive sense. Though he takes chances, he is braced for their possible consequences and is exhilarated and stimulated by their success. He loves the wildlife and respects it. He warms to the native Masai and, one might say, he endures the inquisitive white man.

But my husband and I are alone this hour, without our guide, without our traveling companions, as we walk up the dust path to the fallen tree on the Waso Nyiro River. A bit of the day's history is written on this trail.

A heavy lion print is going our way. Another joins it—and here the two lions commence to run. Toes are splayed into larger, deeper impressions—prints are stretched farther apart. I can see the claw marks in the dust.

Crossing the lions' trail, a single bare footprint of a small child electrifies us.

No, it's a baboon's hind foot, and here is the imprint of the front hand with four fingers straight ahead.

Precise hoof marks of some small antelope have now entered the trail, apparently before the lions passed, for they are obliterated in part by the lion's paw.

Just how near are these lions?

Crossing the path now is the linear record of a mongoose tail, that russet nerve with a head like a magnetic needle. I lean to examine the embroidery of its footprints and pick up, instead, an ossified body of a millipede. It lies the full length of my hand.

We turn off the trail and step into deep grass. Here are fresh elephant droppings. We skirt them uneasily. Our guide has told us that the dik-dik, one of the tiniest antelope, fragile and transparent, with ankles like pistons, seemingly always in silhouette like a Tibetan puppet, asserts himself by building up high mounds of droppings to emulate the elephant. We laugh at the thought.

But we have watched parades of elephants, old and young, lumbering along at the edges of woods. They move softly—elongated into one slate-gray unit, their ears flap slowly like the wings of large birds preparing for flight, their trunks swing and explore, their white ivory tusks glisten in the sun. We would drive downwind and raise our binoculars.

Yesterday, four females with two young, standing in a field across this river, were curling grass into their trunks and stuffing it into their mouths. We were observing them from the open path of our parked car when the largest apparently heard the intonation of our voices. Her ears flew out, up went her head in irritation as her trunk flew down between her great tusks—she screamed and moved toward us. Our guide turned on the ignition.

"Do I hear," he asked slyly, addressing himself to the rear seat, "the human sounds of the jungle?"

But now we are walking through grass, approaching the river thicket. We bend and part the brush along an animal tunnel. With scrutiny and a second's hesitation, we make our way hurriedly to the fallen tree. It is comforting to be off the ground.

Time now is in suspension. It is still the hour of tail-twitching indifference. It is still the hour before the lioness stretches the cords of her neck. It is the hour when the emerald-spotted wood dove makes his sad, soft call in the stillness.

> My Mother is dead,
> My Father is dead,
> All my relations are dead,
> And I am alone—lone—lone.

Time, for us, has strangely become elongated, turning each day into a week of hours. Is this because there are so many chapters to each day? Why has the tempo changed?

True, we have lost the calendar of civilized time, the days of the week, each with its specialized meaning. Still, there is something more than what we have laid aside—there is something we have gained.

Time has become a long, steady stream moving slowly like this river, twisting back on itself into pools of sunshine, then running free into shadow. Our days are like the bend of this river, some spans of an hour cover a hundred miles of revelation.

Upstream, we now hear a pair of bul-bul shrikes synchronizing their duet. Like a swing, one bird carries the melody forward, then the other carries the measure back. A strangely satisfying peace prevails.

Never will I lose the memory of the birds' superb music along the Mara River—a clear note of sunshine, liquid beauty, glory. At dawn, the first birdsong came as a reaffirmation of another day—a bright, supporting, comforting renewal of life after the dark night sounds of predator and prey. It came as the lions were seeking reunion with one another by great throaty rumbles. It came as white follows black, purer and more glistening after the dark. Each morning was a rebirth.

Those nights—each of the sounds from the darkness became personal. The guttural talking of the lions spoke directly to us, making the canvas of our tents seem inconsequential. The penetrating, mournful call of the hyena and the dry, rasping prelude to the screeching of the hyrax locked our breath. Elephants, tangling and shattering the darkness with their power, epitomized a fundamental force far greater than any we had ever known.

"Here I am," I wanted to say.

I am diminished.

I am nothing.

But we have eaten catfish chowder in complacency beside our campfire under a full moon—laughing at the dinner music of hippos grunting and coughing in the river 20 feet away and the sharp-pitched barking of jackals edging the clearing.

Across the river now, a vignette of creation has come into our vision. Climbing straight up a tall tree, a mother baboon holds a newborn baby whose minute, blood-red hands stretch over the maternal body. She stops to rest in a crotch and places her arm about the baby, viewing us with distrust.

Beside us on the fallen tree the baby vervet monkeys, the size of white rats, lie on their backs in a spot of sunshine. Their tiny black-gloved hands and feet, their velvet black face masks, beg attention. Their parents are composed on the roots, like city folk on park benches. These tiny individuals, with codes of propriety, carry egos of sociability and loneliness, gaiety and terror.

Do we hear a leopard cough? The sound comes from the foliage high in the podocarpus tree. Baboons are screaming now in the underbrush—screams of unrestrained anger. Up they scramble into the trees, an epidemic of scolding, quarrelsome voices. Baboons fear the leopard to such a degree that they have learned to imitate its cough.

This evasive, brilliant, decorated cat carries a hypnotic quality with style—leaving a deep imprint on the mind of both baboon and man. Those golden eyes with the needle-prick pupils!

We were frozen with excitement one afternoon, on the edge of the Serengeti, watching a black-and-white-striped tail rise like a banner from the grass—an announcement of silent danger—as a crouched leopard crept past us. The tail had the electric style of a striking cobra.

The words "power" and "mercy" flash before me when we encounter any of the great cats, for they exhibit a natural sense of authority.

Our stormy nights have vibrated with this power, when the slashing wind, the dripping trees and the drum of rain on our tents become but a background to the lion's roar.

I lay on my cot and thought about the gentle encounter we often witnessed between the lioness and the cubs, or two male lions affectionately coming together with a slow rub of their heads. Now, out in the violence of wind and rain and the crack of thunder, they were treading through the wet grass on steady feet, smelling the air, seeking their prey with night eyes and welling up in their throats this great rumbling roar.

One afternoon we observed this power and a form of mercy as we approached a small herd of wildebeests, lined up, seemingly facing an audience while they executed a nervous dance step. We recognized the audience as the ears of a lioness rose from the grass, then another, then three more. They were lying relaxed but attentive to the performance before them. The wildebeests were like live nerves, prancing, but unable to flee.

Our approach broke the deadlock. Suddenly, all the animals turned their heads—the current was cut and the wildebeests were free to gallop up the slope. The show was over.

My husband is nudging me. A movement in the branches holds his interest. In a spotlight of the sinking sun we now see a great luminous coat emerging, a cloak of gold and rust in polygon markings—and high above, the head of a reticulated giraffe is pulling down and munching leaves.

We have recently watched a frieze of some 30 giraffes carrying this royal cloak on their shoulders, their noble necks fluttering with ox-peckers. They were dressed for the opera, and with grace, poise and dignity, they floated in a line of poetry down the vast promenade of the plains, stopping suddenly to turn and slowly gaze back with large, dark, appealing eyes.

In an immortal passage describing the Duchess de Guermantes at the opera, Proust catches the quality we sensed in these aristocratic animals.

> I felt the mystery but could not solve the riddle of that smiling gaze which she addressed to her friends, in the azure brilliance with which it glowed while she surrendered her hand to one and then to another—a gaze which, could I have broken up the prism, analyzed its crystallization, might perhaps have revealed to me the essential quality of the unknown form of life— apparent in it at that moment.

Even in death, we sensed this aristocracy when—driving over Masai charred grass, black as night—we came across an elongated pattern of a total giraffe, stretched out some 20 feet. The strong delicate bones radiated phosphorescent white, the long thin neck, stretched thinner and longer in death, carried the skull with horns of bone, and yes, there lay the coronet.

But Africa is rich in contrasts—and we have experienced more formidable encounters, incorporating neither delicacy nor grace, reducing ourselves to the fragile role and our Land Rover to an insubstantial friend.

The rhino, raising his heavy head from grazing the grass, tossing up the great horn, adjusting the angle of his two-ton body for the straight-line charge—and then, coming. Once, one thundered to within four feet of the Land Rover before our guide lurched the target car into action.

One evening along the Mara River, an incident occurred while driving through a field seeking a herd of buffalo. We wedged the Rover through a thicket of young trees and emerged into tall grass. There, directly before us, a rhino stood with head raised to meet us.

A small sound of concern came from our guide. "I like it better," he remarked as the rhino wheeled toward us like a locomotive, "when the grass is shorter."

We lurched over the uneven land and escaped the rhino's course. Nervously, we were still gazing back at the animal, when we came to an abrupt stop. Crossing the field, a dry wash, referred to as a "donga," stretched like an open trench before us.

"Can we make it?" asked our guide quickly. All of us were out of the car in a second, gravely observing the immediate hazard, then gravely observing the hazard now standing in profile, in the field to the rear.

Yes, we had faith in our little Rover.

The car plunged ahead with courage and down it went, and in a helpless manner, came to a sudden stop.

Standing on the edge of the donga, we viewed the little Rover, which seemed very small and sad. Some 50 yards away, two rhinos were grazing in massive authority—directly in our path.

There was hurried activity among the men as our lovely companion, with snow-white hair and sky-blue eyes, looked at the rhinos ahead, then looked at the rhino behind, then looked at me.

"I'm going to frame it," was her remark.

"What are you going to frame?" I asked, raising the binoculars to bring the rhino into the immediate foreground.

"Your letter," she said. "The letter you wrote suggesting this safari."

We gazed at one another in silence. The next instant, the engine roared, alerting the three rhinos to raise their heads. Our guide, with an effort stored for this moment in time, spun the wheels of the car—and out of the donga it leapt.

We piled back into the friendly little car and drew a great arc through the grass to leave the rhinos in solitude.

Eight birds rode the back of our last rhino as he trotted past an immense gray-molten boabab tree—and was dwarfed by comparison. Both the rhino and the tree came from the same chapter in history. Solitary, in organic splendor, this boabab reached up from a dry rocky floor with fingers to the sky.

It was Manyara, a land of eternal loneliness, a land where man's history seems not yet born. It was an abstract land, the color of tarnished silver, the shape of bleached bones and blunt points with concretions of stone heaped up like graves.

There, at twilight, we sat watching the sky and land meet. Over the soda lake, pink flamingoes clattered as they changed position, slapping the platinum water with their wings. The lake turned satin and the night grew soft and expansive.

We poured our evening drink and watched a yellow-winged bat detach himself from a sparse tree and swoop into the void.

A lion roared close to camp—then was silent.

He roared again, this time closer.

"Oh, lion, where are you going?" I asked.

"He's calling his friends together," said our guide.

"It is only when one does not hear him," he added, "that one might wonder."

So little of the unknown in our lives. But the sky is turning copper now, sharpening a silhouette of two vultures hunched on a bare limb. A covey of vulturine guinea fowl sifts out from the undergrowth near the water's edge.

Once again, an order predictable in its ritual takes place. The approach to the river for a few at a time to drink—the watchful waiting for each to take a turn, holding their heads with a high style, like embellished crooks inset with a burning ruby eye. A luminous blue, taffy-brown and slate-gray sweep up the bank and are propelled forward again for the intuitive procedure.

A hawk is wheeling overhead; circling a tree, he reappears suddenly at an acute angle, dropping among the guinea fowl like an explosion. Out of the confusion, only the hawk remains; stretching his wings, he rises slowly up through the narrow corridor of the river.

On the earth lies a feather.

I slip off the tree trunk to claim it. Eight inches of exquisite understatement—warm in charcoal-brown, pierced by a white quill with opposing elements of design on either side. Is it the symbol of life in Africa, these opposites paralleling one another?

"Beauty," wrote Freya Stark, "walks along the edge of opposites."

Three steady, delicate lines march up the quill on the left— birth—life—death. While on the right, the staccato pulse of life—uneven, nervous and varied—lies in four rows of dots.

So here is the rhythmic harmony—but, as this fallen feather indicates, without a guarantee. Give the guarantee and vitality stagnates.

The nerve song of Africa, found in this unexpected pattern, hidden beneath the vestments of the handsome, vulturine guinea fowl, will be the tangible record of this journey I shall take home.

Turning it in my fingers, I too must accept the opposites in the rhythm as a part of the full harmony. I too must not ask for the guarantee. I look upon the feather with fresh insight.

It is my life.

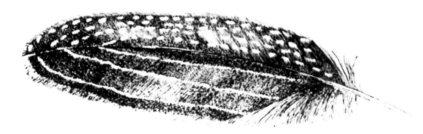

BELONGING

Sigurd F. Olson:
A Voice Crying in the Wilderness

To this poet, a canoe was like a well-worn glove.

WE GREW TO KNOW SIGURD and his wife, Elizabeth, over a period of several decades, but their visit with us in Big Sur left a refreshingly clear memory: They brought wild rice, and hand-printed recipes, which I pressed in the pages of my cookbook; we ate well and sat before the fire, exchanging tales, or "runes." Sigurd presented us with his new book, *Runes of the North*, in which he wrote:

We shall never forget your dream house, and all the
    beauty it encompassed—but more, the warmth
        and love that emanates from it and surrounds
    those who share it with you.
                    —Sigurd and Elizabeth, March, 1967

On our last day together, Sig and I walked along the ridge of the Santa Lucia mountains, directly above our home. It was one of those distinct periods when snow covered the crest and the air was as clear as glass. We found ourselves closely following the fresh tracks of a large cougar. Suddenly, the footprints turned up an embankment, each step slipping back in the snow. We halted, wanting to follow, but respecting his wild freedom, we stood there in silence.

When we made our way home, it was time for the Olsons to hurriedly leave for the airport, but I dared to ask for one more thing. Would he write a few lines on the mountain lion, which I explained was being shot for a bounty. I was desperately trying to win over the state legislature to remove the bounty paid when a lion had been shot.

He went to the desk and quickly wrote what was in his mind, handing it to me, saying, "I don't know whether this will help":

> The mountain lion epitomizes the old wilderness of California. It stands proudly alone at the very apex of a vast assemblage of living things in an interwoven relationship extending over eons of time. If it is lost, we may still have wilderness but one with its uniqueness and savor gone. We need this sense of balance and continuity, the key to the total picture of life as it is.

Yes, Sigurd, your lines were of great help to me and to many others and to many of the legislators when it was voiced at many moratorium hearings in Sacramento. Though upon reflection, many came around to a more favorable point of view, the issue was vetoed by the NRA's influence on Governor Deukmejian. Later, however, Assemblyman Sam Farr introduced an initiative, Proposition 117, 1990, in which the public voted to guard this magnificent animal as well as set aside funds for wildlife habitat each year in wetlands, rivers and forests to share the benefits for all wildlife. I know your good words had a profound influence.

From Ely, Minnesota, Sigurd spent a large portion of his early life in a canoe in the Quetico-Superior region, waging a nine-year battle to preserve what he called "the fatal charm of these unmapped waters." This region embraced 1.4 million miles, and with his poetic voice speaking out, it became a national forest. Here he was to discover the impact of silence and a sense of timelessness and order. "The comprehension of time," he noted, "being endless and relative with all life flowing into its streams."

As I wrote in a review of his book *Open Horizons*, published in 1996: "These years in the wilderness, listening, watching and studying, gradually defined the next horizon which was to give his life a purposeful meaning. 'What a man finally becomes,' he wrote, 'how he adjusts himself to his world, is a composite of all the horizons he has explored, for they have marked him and left indelible imprints on his attitudes and convictions and given his life direction and meaning.'

"Thus it was that Sigurd suddenly knew he was carrying a message, a message to define the meaning of wilderness in all its infinite shades. He dedicated himself to writing, and out of the struggle and discipline came his magnificent writing, *The Singing Wilderness, Listening Point, The Lonely Land* and *Runes of the North*.

"His writing became a strong voice crying in the wilderness, loud in its fighting spirit. It became a powerful national voice in conservation issues of the continent, and from this steady source grew this volume, a book of epic stature, sorting the directives of a rich life and following each back to its wilderness beginnings."

A book that Sigurd returned to again and again was Thoreau's *Walden*, not simply to the reference to nature but also to the necessity of breaking free from worldly expectations and fully living in the moment. Sig was, however, more like John Muir, who was raised by a cruel fundamentalist father but finally broke away from religious dogma and developed a wilderness theology in the high Sierra, where he gloried in the power of nature and was to become the founder of the Sierra Club. Both men reached the minds of the nation and expressed it through their written or spoken words with a deep-seated philosophy. Sigurd spent six turbulent years as president of the National Parks Association and three years as president of the Wilderness Society. For Sigurd, his aim, though not always achieved, was to keep the wilderness bowl unbroken. Sigurd was later asked to join the National Parks Advisory Board, a group with 11 members, formed to advise the Secretary of the Interior, such as Stewart Udall, on park management and proposed additions—considered the most prestigious advisory board in conservation. It was a happy group that met twice a year and included Loren Eiseley, Mel Grosvenor, Durward Allen, Marian

Heiskell, Wally Stegner and Frank Masland. My husband, Nathaniel A. Owings, was one of the early members.

Not long before he died, Sig sent me a photo of his solitary writing shack, covered with snow and ice. Apparently, he had to chop his way through the frozen door. Somehow, it made him think of my minuscule studio over the cliff in Big Sur, where I could hear the whales breathing below. He wrote that he admired my scent of the brine and my passing whales, but that his studio carried timelessness and order. We read in one of his books a meaningful line, which Sig's life was to follow: "When there are no longer any beckoning mirages," he wrote, "a man dies."

In January of 1982, a period of record-breaking cold, with Ely just recovering from a blizzard, 12 inches of fresh snow lay on the ground but the sun was shining. Sig asked Elizabeth to join him to try out their new Christmas snowshoes along the edge of Caribou Creek, a spot he had long described as "a sanctuary of the spirit." Elizabeth had to return home to readjust her new snowshoes and Sig went on alone . . . but fell forward, suffering a fatal heart attack. His son, Sigurd, Jr., who had just returned from Alaska that day, was to go out to Sig's writing shack and find a paper in his typewriter with only three lines:

A new adventure is coming up
and I'm sure it will be
a good one.

The Meaning of Wilderness

Originally presented at the Ninth Biennial Wilderness Conference, San Francisco, California, April 3, 1965.

These two days, we have been turning over in our hands a great rough rock with many facets. It is a treasured rock. We call it "wilderness." Each facet is one variety of this wilderness and the reflection from each facet is a human response to that experience.

There are those of us who look at wilderness, primarily as a dimension, an immensity, a grand proportion—the horizon large against the outline of the dark mountain range. These may be people who work by expansion—and think by expansion, fanning out their interests. It's the broad, deep picture they find rewarding.

Then there are those who turn primarily to the intimate savor of landscape—the detail, the scent of nettle and mint, the lazy buzz of a mountain fly, the careless grace of a flower opening. These people are selective and concentrate their attention, finding their reward in infinite detail.

But neither approach seeks confinement—and both pursue the sense of the unexplored landscape. For each man is his own eager explorer.

It was Rachel Carson who unrolled the long vistas before our eyes and exacted man's place "as a mere moment of time." "This particular moment of time that is mine," she repeated again and again to help us see our place and our role and the perils of our future in the long view. And among us, it is the perceptive explorer who can glimpse this view—can uncover the links and bridges of history and find his own particular place in the moment of time.

Having a landscape to oneself is an exclusive pleasure. Many of us stumble upon this by surprise. Suddenly, it is there—unshared, solitary. One may well experience a reckless moment of freedom or a penetrating moment of understanding. A meaning that was elusive is suddenly clear.

"Promise" is a word I associate with wilderness. Promise and independence are rare qualities found deep in solitude. Promise renews faith. Independence is found only when the sense of belonging is understood.

Sigurd Olson spoke of "the animal oneness with the earth"—the sense of a close relationship, of belonging. How can we recapture this relationship? How can we return to this "oneness"? What kind of ceremony can lead us back?

Could it be the Mountain Chant of the Navajos in their dark circle of branches? The Hopi Snake Dancers at Walpi, stamping on the Sapupal—the door to the inner earth?

The writer Pierre Teilhard de Chardin, that rare soul who could make an experience flare with a presence, said that only if man is receptive—contemplative and aware—can he open these doors to what the universe and life really mean, can he open these doors to belonging. But for most of us, under the pressures and conflicts of human society, it is only in the setting of wilderness that this revelation can unfold.

I myself experienced a form of revelation one autumn morning. In an unexpected moment, I witnessed a thin slice of wilderness—fleeting and brief but filled with a meaning somehow intensified by the counterpart of its setting.

I was on the sidewalk of 55th Street in the heart of New York City. Around me was the noise and confusion, the frantic strain of traffic, all horns and whistles. Tall buildings cast their shadows over the deep chasm of the street. It was the essence of the man-made world.

At that moment, as if by signal, every city sound about me was suddenly hushed. All mechanical uproar was arrested abruptly, as if the power had been shut off. And in the silence of that instant, I heard but one thing—the delicate honking of geese high overhead. I looked up through the slot of buildings to another dimension as a V of geese moved south, calling to one another as they passed out of view. One world gave way to another. It was one of those "burning instances of truth," referred to by Sigurd Olson, "when everything stands clear."

Now Loren Eiseley admonishes emissaries returning from wilderness to record their marvel, not to define its meaning. But I am tempted to call your attention to potent words used by Sigurd Olson: "timelessness" and "majestic rhythms."

Each of you alone can read your own symbols into the incident I have tried to describe. But it seems appropriate, with the dedication of the Dag Hammarskjöld Memorial Grove tomorrow, to close with these lines from his diary:

> A wind from my unknown goal
> stirs the strings
> in expectation.
> Shall I ever get there?
> There, where life resounds.
> A clear pure note
> in the silence.

Not Man Apart

From the Introduction to "Not Man Apart," by Robinson Jeffers in the Big Sur Coast, *edited by David Brower, Sierra Club exhibit format series, 1964.*

THE REGRET WE FEEL FOR FALLEN LEAVES is seasonal, for we know about the imminent renewal of springtime. The regret stirred by the death of a landscape, however, is long lasting and singularly probes our thinking. We may well wonder whether we have taken the immobility of stone too much for granted.

We have taken for granted, for more than a century, the rocky coastlands of the Santa Lucias down the Big Sur coast. We assumed that Rancho San Jose y Sur Chiquito would always stretch south from Point Lobos as a permanent pasture, edged with some 25 miles of shoreline, radiant green in spring, often veiled in fog, parched to gold in summer. There was an inviolable quality to the shore which suggested a birthright for all the people.

Farther south lies a grant of land received from the Spanish throne in the 1830s by a whaling captain, John Bautise Roger Cooper. This holding penetrated the deep forks of the Little Sur River and ran back into the secluded Big Sur Valley, where the redwood groves, the sycamore and the clumps of wind-carved laurel grew.

Forty years passed and new settlers came, staking out their homestead and timber claims, accepting the isolation, hoping they could sustain themselves on ranches and canyons that plunged to the sea. The Pfeiffers, the Posts, the Danis and the Brazil family grazed their cattle, tanned buckskin, raised hogs and shipped redwood pickets and tanbark, proud of their skill in making a lonely living. They bought shoes and yardage goods as personal necessities, coffee, beans, sugar and rice as luxuries.

Their names on the mailboxes still mark the land along the road. But it is a different road. The mail delivery to Big Sur, as Robinson Jeffers described it in 1914, was a dawn-to-dark excursion in a horse-drawn stage. Today, it takes less than an hour. The paved road saved time, but the saving was not free. It was paid for with a corresponding loss of remote wilderness. Pause for coffee in a ranger's kitchen and you may still hear of the whaling days, when grizzlies crashed through the dry sycamore leaves, padding out onto the sands along the Lighthouse Flats to feast on whales washed ashore. You may still hear accounts of the herds of deer moving over the slopes at dawn, or even of the mountain lion quietly following the trail of a returning settler at dusk, a silent shadow, unmolesting.

Or you may recapture the days a hundred years ago when Francesca, the wife of Manuel Innocenti—they were the last Indian family in the area—would walk barefoot through the woods to call on Barbara Pfeiffer at her cabin in Sycamore Canyon. These were formal calls, these meetings of two solitary women, Francesca always carrying her shoes, stopping to put them on before she arrived. They sat in silence, one unable to speak Spanish or the Indian tongue, the other unable to speak English, communicating simply as women.

South of Big Sur, there was only the sea and rugged trails. The Upper Coast Trail laboriously climbed some 3,000 feet to where black oaks, Coulter pines, and madrone topped the ridge and stood dark against the sky.

The Lower Coast Trail threaded its way into redwood canyons, where deer browsed the deep walls of the running streams. It climbed the steep slopes of chaparral out onto the lion-colored hills spotted with yucca. The Castros, the Grimeses and the Torreses built their homes along this trail and lived a life that accepted wilderness as a neighbor.

There was a rendezvous here, where 72 miles of wild coast country lay dazzling in the sun. Rachel Carson called such meeting "a place of compromise, conflict and eternal change." Here sea and land consorted, the seeping moisture in each fold of the mountain range emerged and slipped musically into the continents of kelp. The conflict and change was a natural interplay in the balance of life.

Then came the road.

The new road intruded upon a dynamic ecological balance, divided what had been the indivisibility of the living whole. The old coast road from Monterey to Big Sur, carved out by settlers in 1886, accepted the terrain, explored each canyon, and scouted the ridge. By 1932, road engineers set about to stabilize, widen and shorten, and to span the deep canyon at Bixby Landing with a boldly fashioned concrete arch. South of Big Sur Valley, the road cut hard into the hundred-fold ridges. Blocks of landscape spilled into the redwood canyons or tumbled into the sea 700 feet below. Man's intrusion left erosive scars that would not heal in his time. The earth, jarred by dynamite, still seeks the balance that was and each winter loosens the rocks that block the natural channels on the cliffs, letting a rain of slides thunder over the narrow road. Perhaps the gray fox is agile enough still to climb and descend through the new chaos; few other living things could count on a foothold—not even the chaparral.

The new road brought new settlers, writers, artists, retired or active, industrialists and soldiers who, pricking with the needle of civilization, sought here a partial exile. In their new solitude, all these people had one element in common—the background of the superb landscape.

Twenty-five years after the improved coast road was cut through, the pressure to modernize it began, to realign its curves, to build straight slices for speed that could serve a fast-traveling public—mass-recreation seekers—and the projected real-estate developers. State engineers proposed to put this road into the freeway system. To demand a straight, broad freeway along these unstable cliffs was to ask for disaster—laying waste of environment, of integrity, of natural balance, of the very quality man was willing to travel far to experience. Real-estate developments, out of harmony with the land, threatened to spread down the coast from the north and up from the south to deface the scenery with roadside buildings, with shelves bulldozed into the mountains for house sites, girdling the smooth hills with roads. They planned a phalanx of houses between the road and the sea. Some developers advocated "a reasonable space between houses along the shore." Others advised, "Clear the land of its natural growth to prevent fires." But where, in all this, would the brodiaea hills of my childhood be? Where in the years to come would we find the slopes covered by blooms reflecting the sky in their petals? Where would we see Robinson Jeffers's fields, "veiled in a late rain, wreathed with wet poppies," awaiting the spring?

It was in 1960 that a group of Big Sur citizens called a meeting at the Grange Hall. Recent residents joined with some of the early settlers in sensing that the mountain shoreline would remain the same only if wisdom and foresight prevented misuse. Together they began to view their environment with a new perspective, appreciating that future plans thrust upon their country, plans that would be considered "normal development" in other portions of the state, could here destroy those things they most valued. They set about to defend them.

Out of the movement grew a master plan, encompassing the full length of the south coast. Its formulators listened hard

for the words of the earth. Their goal was to preserve the coast without imposing unjustifiable restrictions on landowners. It was necessary to secure a consensus in the effort to solve a dilemma— the kind of dilemma the American
 of the future will be facing more and more. The master plan called for "clustering" open space, and for controls on future commercial developments.

As a key step, the legislature was persuaded to remove Highway 1 from the state freeway system. It would be, instead, the "scenic highway" prototype for a concept adopted throughout California. Since the road would be inadequate if, in addition to summer tourist travel, large developments fed into it, the master plan proponents set about to control densities and draw up plans for scenic corridors. After two years of controversy, the plan was passed. Its proponents had reached high, and though they had not achieved their highest aims, the final compromise was well worth the long struggle. In the course of the struggle we learned to face and accept new responsibilities in dealing with the land itself, to respect its fragile character, to perceive the meaning of the road.

Those of us privileged to live on this coast, in the immensity of its scope and in its great proportion, enjoy a strong sense of belonging. Perched on the buttresses of the range, we might, with Sigurd Olson, call them "the final bastions of the spirit of man." In our lifetime, may we thus hold them in our hearts.

Four Illusions about Redwoods

Statement made by Margaret Owings, State Park Commissioner, at the joint meeting of the state park commission and the State Highway Commission in Sacramento, California, January 24, 1964.

As I see it, there are four illusions connected with our state park redwoods through which this major freeway is being routed.

There is, for the public, an illusion of depth to the virgin forest along these narrow roadsides—facades, alas, easily fractured.

Three-quarters of our original redwood stands are gone. One-quarter remains; of this, 75,000 acres are in park land. From the remaining privately owned land, about a billion board feet are harvested each year. This means, that in a dozen years or so, no redwoods will be left except those in state hands. This cutting will include many magnificent groves that the public believes already belong to the state. This is the first illusion—the relatively small areas of redwoods in park hands.

The second illusion relates to the damage caused by freeways cut through these circumscribed areas.

First, there is the visible damage of the cut itself and the felling of the giant trees. The public is primarily aware of this. This is not an illusion.

But there is more damage. Not immediately discernible—the alteration of the native environment. *Sequoia sempervirens* are one of the few trees that make their own environment, their own life zone, in which moisture is held in ferns and redwood sorrel, and small streams are tempered and directed by root structures.

Freeways block these natural drainages, develop erosion, cut daylight areas through deep shadowed groves and destroy the adjacent lifezones. Wind tunnels are introduced through formerly protected confines, and bordering trees. Their root structures, already disturbed, are toppled at the first storm. For example, redwoods along the South Fork of the Eel River are doomed to die from the effects of freeway construction adjacent to them.

As it is now, many of the smaller redwood parks are too small to survive, with lumbering and the despoiling of their life zone up to the very inch of their boundaries. A block of trees cannot long withstand the elements and drainage that cut-over lands present to these groves. The addition of freeway construction will spell annihilation.

And then, there is damage in the form of noise. Passing trucks and cars echoing through the woods disturb the highest aesthetic quality that the visitor seeks in a grove. As Brooks Atkinson recently wrote in his column, "The Redwoods are a spiritual resource. They belong to a self-contained world that is silent. Detached. Lofty and overwhelming."

The third illusion also relates to the freeways. A highway spokesman says: "Our interest is in the traveling public and providing a safe highway that will beautify the country." This is a good statement. Yet freeways cutting through redwood parks will cancel these objectives. The traveling tourist is using the freeway to take him to these parks. If his objective is obliterated, he will see a well-groomed freeway but not the beautiful country.

A recent editorial in the *Humboldt Beacon* said: "Our redwood parks will be this county's greatest asset in the decades to come. Any further loss of trees in this area would be a stark tragedy. They must be protected, and we are confident that the engineers of the State Division of Highways are able enough to provide the routes which will give this protection."

And the last illusion violates a trust. Redwoods, more than any parklands in the nation, were acquired through donations from thousands of citizens—people who cared. The Save-the-Redwoods League has collected $10.5 million, which, in turn, has been matched by state funds. These gifts have been made under the illusion that these redwood groves would be preserved in perpetuity from all types of destruction, including the intrusion of freeways.

Nowadays we remake our landscapes. We remove our hills. We redirect our rivers. We fill our bays. But the redwoods are a landscape that cannot be remade.

I would like to see an unbroken policy established by the state of California: That no more virgin redwoods in state parks be cut down for freeways.

After this meeting, the chairman of our commission came over to me and angrily said, "Who do you think you are! Julius Caesar at the Forum?" Yet it was because of these words that Governor Brown announced the next day in the press that he did "not want to see any more redwoods cut down for freeways."

And well might I have turned to our state park commission chairman and quoted a line from Shakespeare's *Julius Caesar*, "O, pardon me, thou bleeding piece of earth, that I am meek and gentle with these butchers!"

LIFELINE FOR
SURVIVAL

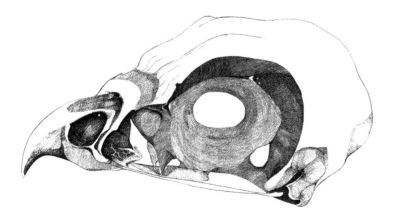

WAPITI: THEY'RE STILL SHOOTING THE TULE ELK

A PAIR OF SHARPLY ATTUNED EARS sensed our presence as the doe elk raised her head above a tumble of rocks and sagebrush. Turning in graceful profile, she rose and picked her way up the draw through the dried twigs of autumn.

The morning sun shone on her reddish-bronze coat, and as she withdrew, her tawny rump held our attention until she was out of sight. Wapiti, meaning "light rump," was the name given to her by the Shawnee Indians. We had seen a tule (pronounced *tool-ee*) elk, a diminutive species named after a Western bulrush.

The striking little *Cervus nannodes* earned its unusual name among the tule marshes of Buena Vista Lake, in California, where the last remnant herd made its final stand in 1873. The San Joaquin and Sacramento valleys no longer contained the herds that Edward Bosqui, a perceptive Californian, had described only 23 years earlier as having "darkened the plains for miles."

The gold rush years had left an infamous record of wildlife treatment. Wanton killing for meat and hides had ravaged and nearly depleted the herds. However, the foresight of one conservation-minded rancher, Henry Miller, had reestablished the last family of this diminutive elk. In the words of Laurens Van der Post, "the tiny seed of the small change in the troubled individual heart" took action and grew.

After Henry Miller found the last remnants of elk on his Miller and Lux Ranch and ordered them protected, a state law was passed supporting his action. The law also made the killing of tule elk a felony.

In 1885, Theodore Roosevelt reported seeing a herd of 28 tule elk. By 1900, the first move was under way to introduce the species to other areas of the state.

Transplanting a number of the animals to Sequoia National Park, however, brought a heavy loss. Man was not prepared to move such free-roaming ungulates; only a calf survived. A series of other adverse transplants followed. By 1915, a total of 146 elk had been placed in 19 parks and reserves, but most of them died. Subsequent transplants were made to Yosemite National Park and Del Monte Park on Monterey Peninsula, with only partial success.

By 1927, the herd at the Miller and Lux Ranch numbered 72, and five years later the state park commission established an elk refuge—a 953-acre, fenced-in area north of Tupman. The enclosure was too restricted for the 75 elk transferred there, however. Artificial feeding diminished their wild character and propagated an unhealthy herd.

Decade followed decade, and the tule elk were without a wild home. "Animals without wilderness," wrote nature writer Lois Crisler, "are a closed book." The elk had protection, but lacked the proper environment.

Then G. Walter Dow, a Californian, obtained permission to liberate the tule elk on the bottom lands of the Owens Valley, owned by the city of Los Angeles for its watershed value and leased to cattlemen and packers for grazing. Mr. Dow believed that the elk would thrive there, where the climate and forage resembled their original environment. With the cooperation and encouragement of Horace Albright, director of the National Park Service, he initiated and financed the transplant of 27 tule elk from Yosemite National Park.

Carefully organizing the move, Mr. Dow built 27 crates. Then he had the antlers removed from each bull elk, to prevent injuries such as those sustained by elk moved in the past. An enclosure was built at Owens Valley to receive the elk, and for 10 days after arrival the animals were watched over and fed before being released. This move proved to be the first successful transplant. The following year, a second transplant brought the number of elk in Owens Valley to 54. The herd flourished; it had found an environment proper to its needs and space to roam. "Someday," Mr. Dow said, "the people of Los Angeles will realize that they own the most unique natural park in the world in the Owens Valley, and it will set it aside as such."

It was appropriate that G. Walter Dow, now 83, was the first person to meet us when we brought our plane down at Lone Pine in the Owens Valley. We had flown from Monterey over coastal ranges heavy with smoke from serious brushfires. The smoke clouds stretched over the valleys to the edge of the Sierra Nevada.

Guided by Mount Whitney's 14,494–foot peak, we dropped down into the Owens Valley under a clear evening sky, entering a self-contained world. To the east, the chiseled bare Inyo Mountains were bathed in an amber glow of sunset. Abruptly to the west, the shadowed jagged slopes of Mount Whitney, in the Sierra, created an almost impenetrable wall. The flat little valley, some 60 miles long and 10 miles wide, lies pressed between these ranges.

Here are both simplicity and grandeur, the primordial feeling of great space encompassed with shadow and mystery. The bottom land is covered with a khaki carpet spotted with saltbush, greasewood and sage, and crisscrossed by the trails of wild deer, elk, cattle and horses. The imprint of man is visible in a few, fenced alfalfa fields. Tamarisk trees in clusters mark the sites of old dwellings, and an aqueduct, stretching the length of the valley, carried mountain water to Los Angeles. The small, dark-green islands are the towns of Lone Pine and Independence, threaded by a highway running north into open range.

As we stepped from our plane to the valley floor, Mr. Dow's hand welcomed us, and his ready conversation steered our thoughts to the great nature reserve at the southern end of the Owens Valley. The Committee for the Preservation of the Tule Elk is working to establish a 240-square-mile refuge there. "It will be a great park," Mr. Dow explained, "where the flora and fauna can live unmolested."

Egrets, blue herons and whistling swans are but a few of the birds that frequent marshlands. Deer, a few bighorn sheep and even a mountain lion contribute to an ecology which the tule elk herds will find natural and helpful.

Three sides of this reserve would have natural boundaries— the dry Owens Lake in the desert to the south, and the two mountain ranges to the east and west. Mr. Dow proposes that there be a drift fence to the north, stretching from range to range across the valley. "These cattlemen keep after the elk herds," Mr. Dow told us.

The grazers shoot at the elk and dog them. They keep them restless and fearful. Since the elk do graze the alfalfa when the natural forage is down, "the cattlemen have a gripe," Mr. Dow concluded.

The tule elk have thrived so well that the cattlemen have repeatedly requested reduction of the herd. In 1943, the state Department of Fish and Game authorized a hunt that took 43 bulls. Four years later, another 107 were shot. The third hunt eliminated 144 elk, and the 1963 hunt reduced the herd by 40. Last October, 50 of the 329 tule elk in the Owens Valley were shot. No hunt is scheduled for this fall.

Under the original cropping theory, the shooting was intended to cull out chiefly the poorer specimens. Actually, however, the hunts have killed six-month-old calves, yearlings and two-year-olds—all healthy elk.

When opposition to the latest hunt failed, Beula Edmiston, a leader in the Committee for the Preservation of the Tule Elk, wrote, "a bit of your heritage and mine dies with the tule elk— this culmination of the past, this indication of the future." We had this thought in mind as we met with Mr. Dow and other conservationists.

We gathered at Taboose Camp, beside a willow-edged stream, with binoculars, cameras, butterfly nets and notebooks. Five jeeps took us up a rough dirt road, threading boulders and sagebrush, brown-headed buckwheat and desert needle grass. Dale McCullough, our guide, working on a biological study of tule elk under A. Starker Leopold at the University of California, has analyzed the forage requirements of the herd, and he pointed out their favorite browse. At Goodale Creek we found clear mountain water, edged by water birch and willow, and the first tracks of the tule elk. The Goodale herd contains some 60 animals foraging over an area of 10 to 12 square miles. They rarely join with the elk in the bottom lands. The structure of the herd, its patterns of browsing and resting and its circuits of movements appeared to be parts of a fine equation.

We observed a herd of 31 animals in the fields of the valley floor. One large bull with a V of magnificent antlers was predominantly the leader. His broad chest was a rich dark brown; his head was held high in dignity and authority while the relaxed herd grazed about him. Younger bulls approached and withdrew in a pattern long established.

As one of our party approached them, the elk raised their heads, the ears of the cows like so many petals, tensed and open, impulse gathering in their bodies. Then, with the old bull in the lead, they ran off, passing before us in silhouette.

"Beauty, not beef, is the wealth of the Owens Valley," Beula Edmiston remarked. It is important to weigh the two sides of the scale when wildlife and the economic interests of men come into conflict. Which is the value most broadly enjoyed and most long lasting? Aesthetic considerations have a practical basis. A society motivated by such considerations is likely to be the most resourceful in the long run. An economic survey might help to prove this point.

"The establishment of a nature reserve could be an economic gain for Independence," said Dorothy Cragen, director of the Eastern California Museum. "It will bring tourists and stimulate business."

An Inyo County supervisor objected. "There isn't a legitimate reason to designate this area as a game reserve," he said. "We don't want to see elk exterminated, but neither are we in favor of having our cattle crowded off the range. "A public resource is at stake," Beula Edmiston replied.

The committee to preserve this resource is awakening public awareness to the cause and attempting to convince the city of Los Angeles that establishing a nature reserve in Owens Valley is in the people's interest.

Meanwhile, the tule elk face an uncertain existence. The elk are the verbal and political targets of "harvest hunt" sportsmen. To assure the survival of the tule elk, the herds need an Owens Valley preserve.

Previously published in Audubon, *Vol. 67, September 1965, pp. 296-98.*

A Moment of Time

My words shall be few—
one, is a word of gratitude for a privilege, the privilege of living in
our land—this century, this decade, this year, this moment of time.

A time—when a condor quill can drift down
     from a great wheeling bird;

A time—when sea otters are rocked in the kelp
     by the moving tides;

A time—one can follow the soft-padded
track of the mountain lion—
     along the streambeds in the Lucia range;

     When one can still hear the circling call of coyotes
     at nightfall on the Anza-Borrego desert;

A time—when the loveliness of motion of the tule elk
     can thread itself out into fields of the Owens Valley.

Yes, we can still find an atmosphere of unlimited freedom
in a living landscape at this time.

Yet, this privilege has become a target
    grain soaked in 1080 poison
    cyanide guns placed by trappers
    pesticides contaminating the environment
    and the gun-in-hand.

And the wild, beautiful habitat of wildlife is intruded by ingenuity, by roads and machinery—the agent is man.

Thus to the word 'privilege,' I add the word 'obligation.'

The obligation not alone to shield the target—but to unblock the moral vision. And this alone can be done by the slow, steady, noble courage of the few.

For only then can man define this privilege which rewards him (in the words of Sigurd Olson) " . . . with a certain feeling of wholeness and fulfillment."

First presented at the Tule Elk Banquet sponsored by the Committee for the Preservation of Tule Elk in Los Angeles, March, 1967.

THE LION IN MONTEREY COUNTY

 A PRIVILEGE TO LIVE IN BIG SUR? Indeed, yes, and one that includes a certain marvel, a certain vision— wherein, to use the words of Loren Eiseley, "the mundane world gives way to quite another dimension." A mountain lion's track, the size of a man's closed fist, pressed on the dusty road near the mailbox, or the curious whistle from this great animal, softly communicating with one of its kin deep in the shadows by the stream below our house—these moments touch the quick.

For 20 years I have been privileged to live in lion country, with its overwhelming sense of the sea below, the dry scent of sage and chaparral on the sun-bleached slopes, the knolls of bay trees and the dark hush of redwood canyons. These secretive cats with the golden-green eyes also know this world thoroughly and patrol each rocky outcropping and each canyon wall more intensively and more intimately than we can conceive. Thus, Big Sur is a shared world, although many are totally unaware that this lion can live harmoniously, but shyly, in proximity to man.

Walking along the ridge road with Sigurd Olson some years ago, in patches of snow and wet black earth, we saw fresh prints of a mountain lion. "A symbol of the past," Sigurd remarked wistfully. "If this is lost, we may still have wilderness, but one with its uniqueness and savor gone." The puma had turned off the road and leapt up the bank. We watched it disappear as if it were still there.

The stunning surprise of a lion's presence has continued to repeat itself over the years on the Monterey Peninsula, whether it be treading the Point Lobos trails after nightfall or moving those elegant shoulders under the oaks in the Carmel Valley. As a young child, I was awakened one night by the scream of a puma beneath my window in the Carmel Highlands—a sound apparently rare, but unforgettable. I spent the remainder of that night rolled in a bundle at the bottom of my bed.

In lion country such as ours, the resident lion population is self-regulating. Females usually breed only every other year and train their one or two kittens for about 20 months, or until they are ready to fend for themselves. These females are the stable center of the population. Solitary males in residence firmly guard their territories against the intrusion of other males, thus limiting the population growth of a given area. These "floaters," or "wanderers," as they are called, may come from some distance or may be two-year-olds which have left their mothers' care and become transients. They move with quiet grace through the brushlands, uneasily seeking to establish a territory for themselves but unable to settle within the well-marked range of another lion. The late Dr. Carl Koford, a research biologist at U.C. Berkeley, estimated that over 30 percent of the lions in Monterey County are transients which sustain high mortality in unfamiliar surroundings. The strong, stable residents occupy the favorable portions of the range, leaving the smaller, semi-isolated animals near the periphery.

At eight o'clock on a December morning, a young, healthy female lion approached a small house on the steep slopes of Partington Canyon in Big Sur. She was drawn toward a litter of puppies playing outside the house, and she quickly pounced on one as she would pounce on a rodent in the fields. She was clearly on the periphery of the range—and she was hungry.

A woman emerged from the house and quickly turned a hose on the lion, driving it up a tree with the dead puppy. People from the ridge soon gathered beneath the tree, where the disturbed puma anxiously watched them. No one had ever seen this close neighbor before. All hoped it could be tranquilized and moved safely back into the wilderness. But when the state Department of Fish and Game warden arrived, he announced that the animal had to be destroyed because it was "depredating livestock" and its action was "abnormal."

The lion was shot, falling to earth with its quizzical look, its proud expression and its golden eyes open—alone against the world.

Present at this unfortunate incident was Kristin Coventry, a resident of the ridge. An excerpt from a letter she wrote to the *Big Sur Gazette* illustrates a heightened public sensitivity:

> We are living on the edge of the wilderness. We are the intruders. We are taking a risk living here and we have chosen to take that risk. I am raising a child here as did the homesteaders and the Indians before them. When the Fish and Game warden pulled the trigger, he shot a much-loved neighbor of mine. He shot the reason I live here—he shot beauty and coexistence and respect.

The crest of the Santa Lucia coast range, stretching from the Carmel Valley south through San Luis Obispo County, has been described as a lion traffic route. But today these travelers, who play a critical role in carrying new genes between widely separated resident lion populations, must cross two wide highways and a divided freeway in western San Luis Obispo County. Recreational roadways and off-road vehicles, reservoirs and housing developments have honed down the lions' natural habitats, confining them "to island regions" inaccessible to lion population exchange.

This animal, which once had the widest distribution of any mammal in the western hemisphere, is practically gone from the entire eastern United States, with the few remaining big cats in the Everglades on the endangered list. In the West and Southwest, they are primarily limited to the rugged mountain areas. Alas, all big cats have declined drastically in number throughout the world, not only because of habitat destruction, but because of excessive trophy hunting and the value placed on luxury furs.

It was in 1962 that a young man was gallantly awarded $100 in bounty payments from the state and county for shooting a fine specimen of a young male lion, treed by his dog not far from our residence in Big Sur. The boy was photographed with his big cat, proud of his trophy—but I was roaring mad! This lion was not to have died in vain. I immediately asked Senator Fred Farr to draw up a bill to stop the bounty. Fifty-six years of bounty subsidies had amounted to $27,500 paid by the state for wanton killing. It was "Mutiny on the Bounty" during the long legislative battle, and in the summer of 1963 we eliminated that cruel relic of pioneer days.

During their former mass persecution by bounty hunters (1907-63), 630 lions were taken in Monterey County alone. When the bounty payments ceased, the total kills in the state numbered 12,461. Studying the records, it is clear that after 1954, bounty kills decreased as the lion population dwindled and in many regions disappeared.

But when the bounty ceased, the mountain lion simply became a nonprotected mammal until, in 1969, the Department of Fish and Game classified it as a big game animal in order to "stop indiscriminate killing." Yet the sale of a 50¢ tag still permitted the hunter to shoot as many lions as he cared to, day and night, with no closed season. In the first year alone, 4,746 tags were sold, but only 84 lions were shot. Yes, every big game hunter wanted to get in on the action, but there were not quite enough to go around.

How many lions were there? "As long as we keep on killing them, there must be lions left," was the laughing retort.

The first state lion hunter, Jay Bruce, had long estimated the number of lions at 600. It was, of course, guesswork, and the number piqued both Fish and Game, who thought there were more lions, and the conservationists, who thought there were fewer. Finally, in 1971, the state legislature directed the department to "ascertain the quantity of mountain lions in the state and determine the best method of providing sound management."

During the following three years, Fish and Game biologists, using trained hounds to track and tree lions, radio-collared 17 pumas and monitored their signals along the Santa Lucia Range in Monterey County. Of the collared animals, eleven were males, including four large residents; and six were females, three of which were probably resident. During the first year of this study, Fish and Game put forward "an initial estimate of 2,400 lions in the state, occupying a summer range of 70,000 square miles."

These Fish and Game figures have never varied, despite estimates to the contrary by the late Dr. Koford, following his three years of lion study—a quiet, persistent approach of slow tracking over 3,000 miles on roads and trails in six study areas in the state. Koford's survey tracked footprints along roads, trails and ridges. He distinguished the numbers and approximate size of pumas and identified individuals by their footprint peculiarities. In India, game rangers carry a "tiger tracer"—a clear plastic sheet in a wooden frame that can be placed over a footprint for tracing and identification.

"I found," he said, "the most consistent mark is the posterior border of the hind foot and the width of its heel pad." Here are some excerpts from his notes:

> During three days in October, 1975, I drove 81 miles through the San Rafael and Sierra Madre ranges north of Santa Barbara. Tracked 48 miles of dirt road and found tracks at seven sites representing four pumas or an index of 8.4 per 100 miles, an indicated monthly track of five per square mile.
> In southeastern Fresno County, on two occasions I found tracks of an adult atop McKenzie Ridge and the same track in Converse Basins seven miles distant.
> One big male at Pozo used the same ridge over a period of at least two and one-half years.

Many ranges had shrunk, Koford found, due to hunting and human encroachment. Kern County south to the Mexican border, the Santa Ynez mountains near Santa Barbara, the foothills west of the Sacramento Valley, and Humboldt County, where lions were once plentiful, and along the big rivers of the southern Sierra foothills all showed marked changes from early records. It was his judgment that an average of 1,000 lions reside year-round in a total area of 15,000 square miles. He believed that 300 females of breeding age carry the population growth, which changes with season and year, depending on varying rates of birth and survival.

Maurice Hornocker, lion researcher, has observed, "hunting can affect not only the temporary number of cats but the population in general. The loss of a vagrant male may be inconsequential, but the loss of a resident female is disruptive."

Public demand brought about protection for the lion in 1972, with a moratorium on hunting with adequate protection for livestock: any lion known to prey on livestock may be killed.

"Livestock losses to lions in California are trivial when compared to losses from feral dogs," reported Fish and Game. "Dogs do 100-fold more damage to sheep than do lions." On our national forest lands in California, about 100,000 cattle and 75,000 sheep graze. Yet losses to pumas are minor, averaging about a dozen confirmed incidents a year, half of which involve sheep.

What does the lion prey on? The average puma kills a deer every 10 to 14 days, according to Hornocker. Taking the less-fit deer strengthens the health of the herd, and the fact that lions keep herds on the move prevents overbrowsing. Other prey consists of wild boar, porcupines, raccoons and rodents, including ground squirrels.

Despite these facts, under the pretense of protecting livestock, state senator H. L. Richardson, introduced a bill in 1980 to reestablish mountain lion hunting in any county where there have been as few as two verified reports of livestock depredation within the last two years. Although Senator Richardson withdrew his bill in the face of overwhelming public opposition and scientific testimony, our small population of mountain lions might again have been sacrificed to the greed of the trophy hunters. And thus the clouds forgather in this initial attempt to break the moratorium which otherwise will continue until 1983.

Those of us who attended the last hearing drove home from Sacramento with some satisfaction but with the full knowledge that we would be returning again and again in the lion's defense.

The next morning, the sun was bright following rains. I stepped outside my front door in Big Sur—and there, only six feet away in the moist soil, were the imprints of a mountain lion—two front paw prints and two deep scratches from the hind feet.

For a moment, everything seemed so right. "The lion has come," chuckled my husband, "to say thank you."

George Schaller, one of the great authorities in the world on the big cats, a scientist trying to weave a lifeline for our remaining wildlife, has written the chairman of the California Senate Natural Resources and Wildlife Committee asking "With what right and what conscience can a few hunters be permitted to shoot the last lions, selfishly obtaining a little satisfaction at the cost of forever depriving thousands of others the pleasure of seeing one of these big cats in the wild?"

Previously published in Pacific Discovery, *Vol. 34, No. 4, July-August 1981.*

THE PERILS OF THE SOUTHERN SEA OTTER

Adapted from an article that originally appeared in The Humane Society News, *1981.*

WHEN A LOW TIDE RISES along the Pacific, with heavy brine slipping out from under the dark cloak of kelp to break on the rocks with a white explosion, one finds a tangible moment to savor vitality. A door flung open to receive the unexpected.

Yes, a moment of strong scent and sound and power—and in its midst, the smallest warm-blooded sea mammal, the little southern sea otter *(Enhydra lutris nereis)* emerges from a dive, its coat a silky sheen, its whiskers fanned like the struts of a parasol, its forepaws firmly clutching a large purple sea urchin. Lying on its back, it threads its way between the kelp fronds for anchor.

These great kelp continents, the giant and the bull kelp (*Macrocystis* and *Nereocystis*), supply nutrition to life forms surrounding them as well as sifting down particles of kelp detritus to the abalone and other shellfish below. Common throughout the otter's range along the California coast, these kelp forests grow at an extraordinary rate and are among the most productive habitats on earth.

The sea otter appears to play a beneficial role in these kelp communities when it preys upon one of its favorite foods, the sea urchin. The urchin population, if left unchecked, feeds on the holdfasts or rootlike structures of the kelp, literally destroying the kelp and subsequently a rich community of plants and animals.

So tightly knit is this evolutionary development that the sea otter is found to be an integral part of the ecosystem. In Alaska, researchers worked in nearshore and intertidal waters comparing the islands where otters were found with those where otters were scarce or absent. They found dense kelp and a rich associated community where otters were prevalent but only scattered kelp and dense carpets of sea urchins where otters were absent. They concluded that the otter was a "keystone species" and that the otter's return from near extinction to its former range was in the best interests of Pacific coastal waters.

Otters have no subcutaneous fat to protect them from cold ocean waters as do other marine mammals, such as seals, so the otter's healthy appetite insures the high food intake necessary to maintain its high metabolic rate and bodily warmth. Its daily diet is made up of a large assortment of shellfish. Forty-five different items have been recorded, including abalone, mussels, crabs, clams and urchins.

Yes, the otter is in competition with man's gourmet appetite for abalone and pismo clams which are managed by the California Department of Fish and Game for sport and commercial fishermen. But more importantly, the food items upon which this little mammal relies for its very existence are becoming exhausted by burgeoning numbers of people.

California's human population, which was less than seven million in 1938 when the sea otter's return became public knowledge, has now reached over 23 million. It's on a collision course with the small population of fewer than 2,000 southern sea otters. As the controversy builds around otters, the word "management" becomes a power play. It does not mean enhancement, but rather it means controlling a species to keep it from interfering with man's ways.

But today, we can still stand on the shore and watch the otter twisting and rolling in the water to wash off food fragments from its furry bib while holding the remainder of a meal in its grasp. The lack of any subcutaneous fat is compensated for by a coat of deep, soft fur with a dense undercoat which the otter meticulously grooms to protect a blanket of warm air trapped among the interlocking fibers.

This cleaning and grooming was described by Jane Bailey in her book, *The Sea Otter's Struggle*:

> Sometimes all four feet work at once combing and scrubbing. The otter's loose skin and long rib cage make it easy for him to squirm and bend in reaching all areas of his coat. So flexible is his body that he can spin his torso around as he lies on his back and still keeps his head and flippers clear of the water.

It was this rich pelt that whetted the fur trader's greed and established markets for luxurious otter fur during a period of 170 years of ruthless killing. More than a million skins were taken between 1741 and 1911, a slaughter of such magnitude that it formed an economic basis for the acquisition of California. In 1872, conversely, the aftermath of the otter trade led Russia to agree to sell Alaska to the United States when it was believed that everything worthwhile had been taken out.

It had been a wild stampede in pursuit of otters as their herds were exterminated, island after island. Alexander Baranov, the most powerful man in the north, had brought the Russian fur trade to its peak and when his rule ended in 1871, he had traded 200,000 pelts worth an estimated $50 million.

In California, it was the Spanish padres who first recognized the value of the otter pelts. From their missions along the coast, they put the Indians to work—clubbing the otters with large sticks. It was reported that a hundred otter skins at a time were hung outside Mission Dolores in San Francisco before shippment to Mexico for trade. This was at a time when the Russians, with enslaved Aleuts, were said to have killed 800 otters in a single week in San Francisco Bay.

My husband and I have been living within sight of a small raft of otters in the kelp beds below our house in Big Sur since 1958. We purchased Grimes Point unaware of the history behind the man who gave this property its name. Eliab Grimes, captain of the contrabandista vessel, the *Eagle*, traded and hunted otters during the first quarter of the 1800s.

In 1833, captain John Rogers Cooper settled in the area and associated with Grimes in the otter trade. On his vessel, the *Rover*, he kept a logbook in which enormous numbers of otter skins were recorded. He stated in this book that he was going to "keep his twelve boats hunting until there is not an otter left in California." He also complained that where he had previously taken 700 otters between San Francisco and Monterey, his last trip had brought him only 32. "As things appear," he noted, "I do not think we will get more than 600 skins in all the coast."

Here we find an early conjecture of "the last 600 otters" out of which only small gene pools, a sparse remnant population of these animals, were to survive. Today, the most recent otter census was estimated at only 2,229 or three-and-a-half times Captain Cooper's rough guess 148 years ago.

Adele Ogden's book, *The California Sea Otter Trade*, lists 181 voyages of identified ships in 61 years (1786-1848), and records the numbers of skins they carried. It is thought that 150,000 to 200,000 otters were taken along the California coast. In 1911, the International Fur Seal Treaty halted any further taking of the sea otters. All were thought to be gone.

The otter's slow, shy return into the kelp beds along the California coast brought castigation and attack by commercial abalone fishermen when they observed that otters, too, preyed upon abalone. One is reminded of an earlier exchange of otter and abalone when, in the 1700s, abalone shells were brought from Monterey Bay to Vancouver Island and the northcoast Indians. Two large shells were traded for an otter skin. These shells apparently were worth their weight in gold. We are reminded of this former exchange when we find the red abalone today selling for more than $100.00 a dozen. Again the value of abalone is putting the otter's life in jeopardy.

The otter's disappearance in the 1800s marked an unnaturally large increase in the population of shellfish. When commercial exploitation of abalone began, this industry harvested a field that was abnormally abundant, untouched by otters and almost untouched by man for 40 years. In the Monterey area, they landed an excess of 42 million pounds before the beds were depleted and the industry moved south to Morro Bay. They left behind millions of large abalone shells in mounds. These tell their own silent story of excessive human predation.

Yet, the California Department of Fish and Game states: "It's clear, that within the sea otter's stabilized foraging range there can be virtually no human harvest of abalones." How can we value this statement when during prehistoric times immense numbers of otters were foraging for shellfish in the intertidal and subtidal waters of the coast, while at the same time, during this long, long period, Indian middens—heaps of discarded abalone shells—leave records of heavy harvests of abalone.

"The amount of abalones in coastal middens is fantastic," says Dr. Sylvia Broadbent. "Some are over an acre in extent and 20 feet deep, lining the coast from Humboldt to San Diego."

But with the return of the otter, noted in 1938 when over 100 otters, the first large herd reported since 1831, were seen and photographed rafting at the mouth of Bixby Canyon on the Monterey coast, the abalone fishermen rose up in indignation. Some of these otters were to gradually move south toward the Morro Bay red abalone waters that were claimed by commercial fishermen as their own.

In 1957, the abalone harvest exceeded five million pounds, a major catch which was almost equaled in 1966. After this, the divers returned to their abalone beds and found them depleted—not just within the otter's range but outside as well. Looking for a scapegoat, they claimed the sea otter was the culprit. The industry pressed for legislation to provide that otters could be "taken" outside their refuge. Strong public response led by Friends of the Sea Otter opposed this measure and the bill was not passed.

IN 1941, the California legislature established a sea otter refuge to protect otters from firearms, not to limit their range. As the otters slowly expanded their range, the refuge was enlarged to cover approximately 100 miles. During this period, the sea otter was under state control, but in 1972, the responsibility was taken over by the federal government through the enactment of the Marine Mammal Protection Act.

This act, broad in its scope, was designed to reduce the alarming worldwide depletion of marine mammals. The Marine Mammal Commission was established with a committee of scientific advisors to counsel both state and federal agencies on scientific and policy matters, and to monitor and oversee the programs.

The passage of the Endangered Species Act in 1973 became a further protective measure for the southern sea otter. In January 1977, the U.S. Fish and Wildlife Service designated the southern sea otter as a "threatened species" on the grounds that its present range covered only 10 percent of its former area; that it represented less than 2,000 otters and that otters were jeopardized by oil spills and by competition with man. These factors, they pointed out, made the species "particularly vulnerable to any sort of disruption."

Improved equipment for diving was used by the commercial abalone industry following World War II, making it possible for the divers to remain underwater for prolonged periods with their wet suits and air compressors and 300-foot diving hoses. The abalone iron, or "bottom bar," was employed for prying the abalone off the rocks.

How does this compare with the sea otter and its unique ability to use a rock tool selected with apparent care for its shape and size for the job at hand? Divers have reported watching otters underwater choosing such a rock to carry to the surface, then, having used it to crack open a shell, returning it to its former location to retrieve again and again.

Abalone is loosened from its hold on a rock by hammering with this tool, often breaking a hole in the center of the shell. When it is borne to the surface, the tool is not needed because the edible body of this large snail is easily accessible.

Surfacing from a dive with a clam or a mussel between its nimble forepaws, the otter removes the rock from the loose fold of skin under its armpit and places it table-fashion on its chest, then begins cracking the shell against the rock until the broken pieces are easily edible.

People grow to recognize this sharp tap-tap even at a distance. On quiet days and nights, when the sea and winds are silent, I have caught that particular sharp sound rising from the ocean 600 feet below our house in Big Sur, and with ears adjusted, one may also pick up the shrill birdlike cry from an otter pup seeking its mother.

What happens during storms to the small pups clutched by their mothers? How can the mother leave the pup when she dives to feed? Only four or five pounds at birth, it can be washed ashore and stranded by receding tides. Its piercing cry can be muted by the roar of the sea. What happens then?

I had the good fortune to observe over a period of time, a sea otter which had given birth to a male pup near the Coast Guard breakwater in Monterey Bay. This perfect little specimen asserted itself with a shrill voice and went through painful adjustments to the constant movement of waters and frightening periods of apparent abandonment when its mother fed. The pup soon attracted a steady audience from the Coast Guard, scuba divers, students and tourists.

Each morning, the mother would ferry the pup to the breakwater, dislodge it from her body and dive to seek invertebrates hidden in the crevices of the rock wall. The baby rose and fell with the incoming waves, screaming and scanning the water for its mother. If she surfaced without food, she moved quickly to her drifting baby, drawing it back to the spot she had previously left it, and then, with a graceful turn of her body, she dove again.

Returning with a small abalone from which she removed the meat, she placed the empty shell on the baby's chest and he played with it before losing it overboard. Later, we were to see the pup accept its mother's offer, immediately grasping the shell with both paws, then tipping it to drink sea water. As weeks passed, it imitated its mother more and more, pounding her gifts of shells with a firm paw.

The most satisfying scene took place when the mother had fed adequately and turned her body, lifting the clinging pup to her chest. She groomed the mass of fur, causing it to stand up like thistle-down, then, reversing the little body, she placed its head on her nipples. Contentment was apparent as the mother stretched her neck and head in a kind of exultation with her forepaws held high.

This mother and pup, like all otters, are tragically susceptible to oil spills, especially in the southern portion of the range. Oil terminal activities, oil tanker traffic and, in the event of offshore oil drilling, a permanent threat lies in wait for the entire sea otter population along the California coast. South of Morro Bay near Point Buchon, the southernmost female rafts are found, and mothers and pups are glimpsed nestled in the kelp. North from Morro Bay at Piedras Blancas, Fish and Wildlife biologists are studying and tagging otters. This is an area where females remain most of the time and males make 50- to 60-mile trips from the south to breed with them.

The peak of pup births occurs in February and March, although small pups are seen year-round. Twenty to 21 pups per 100 animals is about the maximum count during peak months along the total otter range. In the southern periphery of the range, 150 to 200 animals, mostly males, have been counted during the winter months.

In these winter months, when there is the greatest likelihood of an oil spill, the oil drift would reach otters, drawn together into large rafts in the remaining storm-torn kelp beds. Wind, waves and currents could spread oil over vast distances of the coastal waters, soiling the furry bodies of the otters as well as contaminating the invertebrates on which they feed.

Friends of the Sea Otter has taken a resolute stand on the threatening issues that plague the very existence of this little sea mammal—once sacrificed in man's frantic rush for fur, then unjustly attacked by man's unwillingness to share the shellfish, and now facing a far-reaching jeopardy to its habitat and its life by man's reckless drive for oil.

We must remind ourselves that the California sea otter, long separated from its Alaskan cousins by 1,700 nautical miles, represents a sanctity of life here on our shores. More than that— in spite of the dark and troubled threats that deeply worry us— the mounting concern for the survival of the sea otter illustrates something fine in a humane response. During these times of abuse and wanton killing of wildlife, it represents a true hope for conservation.

Friends of the Sea Otter was founded in 1968 when the California sea otter population was a fragile 562. From that first year when the otter truly needed a friend to this present time, an ever-growing body of supporters has been unswerving in a single-minded objective to see that the otter gets equal time and consideration in arriving at the solutions to the complex problems of man and the sea.

KINDRED SPIRITS

Sharing Life with the Stegners

It was in the early 1960s when Nat and I first crossed paths with Wallace and Mary Stegner. "A common interest in environmental issues threw the four of us together," Wally would later write.

We had heard Wally speak several times at Sierra Club conferences, and I was particularly moved by his childhood memories of a settlement out on the flat prairies of Saskatchewan, in Canada. When he was a small boy, the family lived in an old train with "real glass windows," dragged off the rusted tracks of a defunct railway line. The prairie grass was tall and windswept, and at one point, he recalls, he was given an aged black-and-white pony no one wanted. It was his very own, and he led it around by a rope. One day it disappeared, and he looked everywhere for it until he came to the dump, where he saw it lying on its back with its feet in the air, dead. His childhood was tempered by experiences like this. He carried throughout life the scent of wind willow, which, when he deciphered it, flooded him with memories.

We actually met Wally and Mary one afternoon at Ansel Adams's house in the Carmel Highlands, in a room filled with talented people—fingers playing the grand piano, photographs by Ansel lining the walls, articulating the gleaming rock and shadows of Half Dome. Virginia Adams, with a smile of welcome on her face, was seated quietly beside a large window facing a rocky slope dense with succulents, bits of paintbrush and sprawling ceonothus. Ansel was standing under the big drum over the fireplace, and yes, there they were, the Stegners, "the inseparable two." We were caught by something in them, felt a kinship, and urged them to come down for a visit to Wild Bird. "Come for dinner and the night," we said, and they did.

The Stegners themselves lived in Los Altos, where Wally was close to Stanford and his literary classes, and not far from San Francisco or the airport from which they were constantly flying for lectures or to visit with his publishers, or sometimes just looking for a new place to live.

They had a little place in Greensboro, Vermont, and invited us to come for a visit. His little notes always reflected his dry sense of humor: "Pretty soon snow. Pretty soon Stegners come home, because our waterline lies right out on the ground and our joints lie right out on the surface of our skins. Look for the old couple with canes."

As time passed we found ourselves spending more time with them, traveling with the National Parks Advisory Committee, based in Washington, D.C., but covering a broad scope of old parks or potential parks with a talented group of conservationists, including Sigurd Olson (Wilderness Society), Marian Heiskell (*New York Times*), Laurence Rockefeller (philanthropist), Durward Allen (wolf expert), Loren Eiseley (writer), Mel Grosvenor (*National Geographic*), and others. The group was always refreshing, but deep and sometimes very funny.

One night in the West Indies, we were all on a small island trying to cross from one side of the island to the other but found only one cab. It was raining, and we all tried to pile in, sensing that our driver was a wild, happy man in a great hurry. We stopped worrying when a lovely, small voice from Marian Heiskell, crunched in between so many bodies, suddenly announced, "Yes, we're going to turn over and burn, but let's make it clear that they'll keep all of our ashes together." And then a masculine voice chimed in, "Well, we've got to vote now on which park we'll be buried in."

In 1973, Wally was to receive an award at the Environmental Defense Fund Annual Dinner. He couldn't be present, and I was asked to say a few words about him.

> There is an old Spanish greeting that goes, "Tell me your life and miracles." I associate this greeting with Wally, who has the ability to read into the experiences of life with moments of insight during casual encounters, and the skill to sense these moments when they come: "And the world rises before one's eyes!"

After Wally heard what I said, he wrote to me: "You are a sketch, no, maybe a finished work. If I'd been at that dinner, I'd have blushed a deep crimson and left the room coughing, and would have liked myself all the way."

Late one summer, Wally and Mary came to visit us in Jacona, New Mexico, for 10 days. It was to be a period of rest for all of us. We called our place *Festina Lente*, which means "make haste slowly." During their visit, we drove them across a bridge over the Rio Grande to explore on the other side, up into the Sangre de Cristo range, where the villages were individually apart from the world and filled with nostalgia and a sense of prehistory.

Off we went the next morning up through Chimayo, with its town center, so worn down that some 18 or 20 adobe homes had almost returned to adobe dust.

As we drove up the road through Truchas, few people were in sight. We passed several graveyards filled with crosses among dried grasses and a few plastic flowers, apparently long forgotten. This was the town where Robert Redford was to film his movie, *The Milagro Beanfield War*, and where our old truck, with the bullet hole through the windshield, became one of his chief props. But as we drove up the single road with the Stegners, we were to meet only one truck, plummeting down toward us with the horn blaring and bottles being thrown out of the windows.

Nat turned our car about, and we climbed the mountain road toward Trampas. This town, I explained to the Stegners, is a happier town. Besides, it has a house for sale which Nat has been on the verge of buying for years.

We took Wally and Mary up to the house that Nat had always dreamt about. It was on the steep side above the narrow sunken valley into which all waters flowed and where a few cows browsed among sheep. It had a stone terrace on which the rooms and doors faced out into the sunshine, and Nat would go up there to stretch out and rest or nap. Mary thought about it for awhile but finally said to Wally, "You know how much we love to be alone, but I don't know if I want to spend the rest of my life looking down on those sheep and half-dozen cows." Wally nodded. "No, it doesn't answer for us, but it sure would give me an uninterrupted time to write."

We were to cease looking for another Stegner house, since Wally had received a request from his publisher that he change the ending of his latest book, *Recapitulation*. He took it in stride, other than the fact that he had no typewriter, but I brought out my own antique portable, a gift from my father on my 16th birthday in 1929. Wally responded with a laugh and a note of elation in his voice as the little keys snapped up and down and the novel shifted its final chapter to suit thoughts by someone other than himself.

After they departed, Wally wrote a letter of appreciation for their visit. "I sent thee late a rosy wreath entitled Mormon County, not so much honoring thee as fulfilling thy expressed and probably perverted desire to read it. Those ten beatific days while we made haste slowly."

Since we had named our place *Festina Lente*, we hoped we could live up to it, but that "slow pace" had been hard, since Nat and I were almost always on the go. But Wally went on to embroider our Latin name by saying, "I could quote you Catullus: *Lenta, lenta currite, noctis equi*," adding that it translated, "Run slowly, slowly, horses of the night." Would that we had named it thus, for throughout the night, freerunning horses passed our house a dozen feet from my bedroom's open window.

Would that we could have enjoyed more of the Stegners' moments.

Early in the 1980s, the Mountain Lion Foundation sought to hold a large and popular auction in San Francisco to raise funds for its work. I telephoned Wally, who had just returned from a trip to the east coast, but he was terribly ill, and had taken to his bed with a temperature of 102.° Still, I couldn't give up on my request, which was that he write a page about the California mountain lion. I told him it would be read aloud, as a centerpiece, during the auction, and then would be auctioned off itself.

Feebly, Wally replied, "Margaret, I can't do it. It's hard for me to even think, let alone remind you of how little I know about the cougar."

I hurriedly sent him a factual article, knowing full well he could turn facts into magic. Too weak to refuse, he finally agreed.

When the auction took place, Wally had no way to send his article to San Francisco, so he came himself, feeling, of course, quite miserable.

I called Wally the morning after the auction to let him know his magnificent article was the best piece of writing he'd ever done, and the impact of his words was far greater than he could know. I also suggested that perhaps he should write more often when he had a temperature of 102!

MEMO TO THE MOUNTAIN LION
by Wallace Stegner

ONCE, IN EVERY CORNER OF THIS CONTINENT, your passing could prickle the stillness and bring every living thing to the alert. But even then you were more felt than seen. You were an immanence, a presence, a crying in the night, pug tracks in the dust of a trail. Solitary and shy, you lived beyond, always beyond. Your comings and goings defined the boundaries of the unpeopled. If seen at all, you were only a tawny glimpse flowing toward disappearance among the trees or along the ridge of your wilderness.

But hunters, with their dogs and guns, knew how to find you. Folklore made you dangerous, your occasional killing of a calf put a price on your head. Never mind that you preferred deer, that your killing of livestock was trivial by comparison with our own dogs. You were wild, and thus an enemy. You were rare, and elusive, and elegant, and thus a trophy to be prized. Under many names, as panther, catamount, puma, cougar, mountain lion, you were hunted to death through all the East and Midwest. The last catamount in Vermont was shot more than a hundred yeas ago. You persist in the Everglades only because a national park official quietly released a pair of you to restore the life-balance of that fecund swamp.

In the mountain and plateau West, a remnant population of you persists, in the pockets of wild country off the edges of settlement and too rough for off-road vehicles. If you kill a calf or a sheep, the permit hunters still exact a more-than-eye-for-an-eye vengeance, but in California, at least, a moratorium on ordinary hunting has let your numbers stabilize. The Fish and Game people say there are 2,400 of you in California. A better guess might be 1,000. But a remnant. There is a chance you may survive.

You had better. If we lift the moratorium that has helped to save you, we are insane. Visiting Africa, 20th-century Americans are struck by how poor we have become, how poor we have made ourselves, how much pleasure and instruction we have deprived ourselves of, by our furious destruction of other species.

Controls we may need, what is called game-management we may need, for we have engrossed the earth and must now play God to the other species. But deliberate war on any species, especially a species of such evolved beauty and precise function, diminishes, endangers and brutalizes us. If we cannot live in harmony with other forms of life, if we cannot control our hostility toward the earth and its creatures, how shall we ever learn to control our hostility toward each other?

Written by Wallace Stegner, Los Altos, CA, 1981. Copyright William Newson. Reprinted with permission.

Images of Rafting the Grand Canyon

Lee's Ferry, Arizona—warm heavy sky, loose torn clouds. People standing around under the willow while the boats are being loaded. Piles of boxes, kits and bags interspersed with orange life jackets. Silence to the point of echo. Hollow sounds of thudding in boats. A yellow bird sings in the willow. Nat, looking like Smokey the Bear, raises his binoculars towards the bird. Shadows are shifting. Martin Litton is putting on his new sneakers. Then he hurls a pack containing the Stegners' precious goods toward the dock and hits the water instead. Plastic bottles with the bottoms cut out are thrown into the boats for bailing. Paul will be our oarsman, he says the boat is tippy and insists on a second pair of oars. Our boat is called *The Music Temple*. Martin is rowing the dory with the Stegners. Their boat's name is *Diablo Canyon* (a nod to places not saved by the Sierra Club). We have four dories and a rig of rafts.

"It's here! The moment of truth is here." A cicada buzzes. "Row, row, row your boat!" Clouds are gathering. A can of pop floats by. No noticeable current as yet. Sound of rapids ahead and bird song above the low voice of the rapids. We are entering the rapids sideways—now our nose is straight ahead. "A fast chop," says Paul. A water ouzel scoots directly across our bow. Cliffs about 100 feet high—layers of brown. Very quiet, drifting like a canoe. Now, a roar approaching—background music for bird song.

Floating in circles along a glassy surface under Navajo Bridge. We are soon to approach our first real rapids, Badger Creek, but for now nothing except a moving floor of water. Badger is smooth water pouring over a dome to a lower level and into hit-or-miss waves, rocking and tearing at us. Paul handles our boat perfectly.

Several miles further, we pull over to camp before tackling Soap Creek Rapids. The water is high as the day comes to an end and the rapids apparently are torrential. We all find spots in the sand and rocks to bed down. We eat our one meal of fresh steaks, canned tomatoes, canned potato salad and canned pears. I adjourn to my bed and stillness lies softly over us, a cicada.

The next morning, we approached a roar unlike any I had ever heard. It sounded like a jet flying low over the canyon wall. When we pulled over to shore and climbed onto a rock, we saw what obviously appeared to me to be the route to oblivion.

A frame of sky—lying on sand in a clearing of tamarisk, the river rushing, roaring and whispering by. Red rock fortress walls climbing perpendicular 800 feet from the river. Behind us is red rock in horizontal stripes—with a loop of canyon. Lying in the sand, looking up at the night sky. It is framed as if to intensify a luminous edge. The constellations, the Big Dipper, slipping over cliffs behind us. A criss-cross of planes and satellites appear to thread their way through the stars. *This is it. This is here.* The world goes on outside this frame, quarreling with greed and violence, but here, the sound of the river goes on, running high at night as more water is released, diminishing in the morning. Sometimes in the night one hears a crescendo in the small rapids running by our lip of sand and rock and tamarisk sprout.

I am aware of silhouettes—one massive form against the other—and we are so small. A blue grosbeak alerts us with calls. The colors as we pass are rose, pink, flesh—then ocher, olive green, brown and gray. The river glides, pink over pink sand, jade green in the depths, and white over the rapids. The orange life jacket represents the human element. The broken oar at Soap Creek Rapids. I see broken oars splintered and curling on the sandy beaches of the coast. When did they break and in what spirit were they tossed to sea? I have heard the friendly clink and clash of oarlocks on a mountain lake and the hollow thump as wood hits a pier, but never before have I looked to an oar as the key to Soap Creek Rapids.

Our dory with oarsman, Paul, slides over the pointed glassy tongue of water as it pours into the broil of confusion. As we hit the first trough we are threatened by seven-foot waves, from two directions. At that moment, trying to avoid a deep whirlpool, the right oar and oarlock rise from the boat and become powerless. One stroke by our oarsman, in an attempt to keep from capsizing, and the oar snaps in two. Now water is simply draining over us. The boat is filled with water above our waists. Too much is happening to be frightened. Nat has the presence of mind to unhook a spare oar with its oarlock and hand it across to Paul. He fits the oarlock in, and following several slaps of harsh water, we dive through two more troughs on our side and straighten out, the river still pouring over us. The next pull on the new oar snaps it, but the hurdling waves diminish; we drift down river and wash up on a sandy beach. We climb out of the water-filled boat. I feel the impact in a giddy way as our feet touch ground.

It was a magnificent experience, rough waters, then glassy calm, then tumbling and drifting. We saw only one other raft over the course of many days. It was called *The Pig Pen*, its oarsman, a huge man with a long fuzzy beard, rowing two couples, two handsome men and two beautiful women. Coming around a bend of the river we suddenly viewed a huge red rock amphitheater like the stage of a great opera house. Our companion, San Francisco author Harold Gilliam, dashed up the center of the stage and began to sing an aria of *La Traviata*. *The Pig Pen* floated into view and one young woman, in pink shorts and petal-brimmed hat, rose and answered Harold's aria— an opera singer's sanctified moment.

At the close of our trip, Wally stepped out of his raft, remarking, "A river is always passing, but is always there."

EARTH'S WISDOM

The Wildlife Ethic of Maurice Hornocker

Cougars and Siberian tigers are wild and free, with a relentless drive for life. These big, magnificent cats are a proud presence, rarely seen by man unless chased by barking hounds.

I might not have met Maurice Hornocker if a mountain lion, which frequented our canyon and house in Big Sur, and which we happily considered a part of the family, had not been shot by a young man whose dog had chased it up a tree. For this "deed" the hunter was awarded a bounty of $100.00 from the state and $50.00 from the county. To say that I was distressed beyond measure was an understatement, and I urged a bill into the legislature to halt the bounty system. It was halted by a moratorium which reoccurred every few years until our last governor (George Deukmejian), with the backing of the National Rifle Association, vetoed it. During these dozen moratorium years, Maurice guided us with his words of wisdom.

During his doctoral studies at the University of British Columbia, he began his cougar project, explaining to his questioning associates, "Cats hold a special interest for me because they're at the top of the evolutionary scale. They're the epitome of a finely tuned hunting animal."

Accompanied by a houndsman, he learned to dart and tranquilize the treed lions, climb the tree, rope them, lower them to the ground, check their health and age and fit a radio collar around their neck before they emerged from sedation. This work was carried on in snowbound midwinter within 200 square miles of wild, rough terrain where they captured every cougar, year after year.

He established the Hornocker Wildlife Institute, where he trained students in wildlife research and situated his wildlife headquarters at the Running Creek Ranch on the Selway River in Idaho. It can only be reached by plane or by trail, and is surrounded by a great assortment of wildlife.

I was pleased to be taken there for a splendid gathering of scientific minds to review their work and pool their achievements to better understand the ecological imports. It was a place so apart from the world that probing minds could not be pulled aside. I talked with John Craighead, author and naturalist from that famous family in Yellowstone, whom Hornocker had told me, "taught me most of what I know." It was like a stream whose force is flowing, "a way of life," he said.

One of the Hornocker Wildlife Institute's many projects was an experimental research study on the translocation of 13 lions. They were moved more than 320 miles through rough circumstance and released in totally new habitat. Those of us involved in saving the species had urged the translocation of a problem lion which might threaten the lives of children playing near a lion habitat. It was an uneasy experiment and not always respected by the bureaucrats. We wanted to find out how far the lions had to be moved from their home base, so that they did not return.

The thirteen pumas were taken from the White Sands Missile Range in the San Andreas Mountains in New Mexico to northeastern New Mexico where the terrain was very different. Radio-tracking revealed that three lions died, two were killed by a resident lion and one was killed by another animal it was hunting. One returned the 320 miles to his original home. One translocated female became pregnant and gave birth to five kittens. The five remaining lions were apparently unsettled.

Besides focusing on mountain lions, the Running Creek Ranch was a center for research on brown bears in New Mexico, jaguars in Brazil, and even whooping cranes. In 1975, the cranes were saved from extinction by cross-breeding them with sandhill cranes. The center also fostered studies of bobcats, wolverines, river otters, beavers and badgers.

"Wildlife, wherever it occurs in the world," stated Dr. Hornocker, "acts as a barometer of environmental health. We at the Institute pledge to continue exploring the interwoven complexity of the natural world, and how this knowledge can aid in the conservation of our precious wildlife, as well as we humans."

In the 1990s, the center's research focused on the largest tiger in the world, the Siberian amur, almost gone in Russia. The Siberian amur, in the evolutionary stream of life, was the first form of this species, which, as the landforms of the world shifted into island and massive countries such as China and India, gave birth to subspecies. Its numbers declined rapidly following the swift change of Russia's government and the ensuing massive cutting of forests and the poaching for tiger skins and body parts for markets in China and Korea. In the 1,400-square-mile Sokhote-Alin Biosphere Reserve, established in 1936 as a wildlife habitat, the total dropped to about 50 tigers.

By 1992, Hornocker and his institute associates, Howard Quigley, Kathy Quigley and Dale Miquelle, brought their Russian colleagues Igor Nikolaiev and Evgeny Smirnov to Running Creek Ranch, establishing friendship and understanding seated around a big fire, surrounded by towering stone mountains. They carefully mapped out a plan to submit to the Russian Ministry of the Environment in Moscow to expand the reserve to incorporate critical tiger habitat, to control forest cutting and the building of roads for trucking and poaching. They introduced Hornocker's technical skills to dart tigers, sedate them and place radio collars around their necks, to know them as individual animals, learning their habitats as the seasons change. In short, they drew the Russian biologists into the close-knit Hornocker tiger team. They secured funding from organizations and private gifts in the United States, and set about moving into the tiger habitat and introducing technical skills to dart tigers, sedate them and place radio collars around their necks to learn their transient or residential patterns.

Sadly, it was not long before they lost their first "study tiger," named Lena, whose unweaned cubs were hiding in the snow close to where their mother was killed—her radio collar slashed from her throat, still sending out transmission messages. The poachers were never apprehended.

The team found the famished cubs and two of them lived to be nourished and strengthened for a long air trip to Omaha, Nebraska where a zoo with other Siberian tigers was able to medically care for and nurture them. The Hornocker biologists knew that if the species was going to survive every single animal in the wild would have to escape poachers and continue to breed.

May I tell you about a circus down at La Paz, in Baja California? A tiger that one might see in a circus is a victim, raised cruelly for entertainment because their power is so much greater than any man can compete with. My husband and I had driven down to that settlement to join friends for a yachting trip among the islands of the Sea of Cortez. Arriving before them, we wandered into the outskirts of town, noting a large poster of a tiger. We moved towards a big tent. Somehow, neither of us were thinking of the tiger personally and we were casual when we spoke—why not go in? But apparently, every seat was taken, then the ticket men called us back. They could give us the "best seat in the circus."

Unthinking and light at heart, we agreed and were led into the big tent at ground level where a wooden stage was raised about three feet from the earth and we were seated with our knees almost up against it. The circus band stopped playing and the stage was cleared of all living things. Two little boys, carrying garbage can tops appeared and bent down and pushed their way into this narrow aperture between our knees and the wooden stage. Suddenly, a man dressed like a Roman warrior came across the stage holding at arm's length a steel rod hooked to the collar of a large, powerful tiger. The man was not leading the tiger (nor would he have been able to), the tiger was pulling him in a straight line toward our seats. No cyclone fence guarded us—nothing guarded us! The boys, holding their garbage tops like shields, rose slightly and threw handfuls of bones at the tiger's mouth as it rose on its hind feet and clawed the air. At that moment, two men dressed in black loudly ran down the bleacher steps behind us, banging together large black iron pots which they concentrated directly above our heads. The din of this sound was nothing compared to the tiger which let out a roar so loud that the audience screamed and we were in a state of drained terror.

Clearly the warrior needed help and another warrior holding a similar rod raced across the stage and fastened its hook on the opposite side of the tiger's collar. The tiger, wild with rage, stood on its hind feet, switching, choking and defending itself with its front paws. It made a sound, louder and more disastrous than anything on earth, "aroom, aroom, aroom!" it roared.

The scene was a crime against life—cruel torture, incredible indignities with its great paws stretched out for survival. My husband and I broke from our seats and dashed for the exit.

This was a form of torture the humanoids from the Dark Ages might have used with a prehistoric tiger—not a circus entertainment device in the 1970s, a malicious crime that we shamefully had paid to witness. Where is morality in the minds of human beings and where is a strong ethical standard for treating, not just one another, but all living animals well?

> In a world older and more complete than ours, animals move more finished and complete, gifted with extensions of the senses we have lost or never attained, living by voices we shall never hear. They are not brethren, they are not underlings; they are other nations caught with ourselves in the net of life and time, fellow prisoners of the splendour and travail of earth.
>
> —Henry Beston

Archibald MacLeish

"To see the earth as it truly is, small and blue and beautiful in the eternal silence in which it floats, is to see ourselves as riders on the earth together, brothers on that bright loveliness in the eternal cold—brothers who now know they are truly brothers."

—Archibald MacLeish

WE LOST THE POET Archibald MacLeish in April of 1982, as he approached his 90th birthday. But we have not lost his eloquent, visionary thoughts, such as those he expressed when the first astronauts reached the moon in 1969 and turned their gaze back to our little planet. For a concept thus described is desperately needed this very hour to remind us that we are all "riders on the earth together"—not simply man with man but man with nature, with respect for the land, clean air and clean waters essential to all forms of life. Yes, we are "brothers"—environmentalists, conservationists, defenders, preservationists—all campaigning together against energy programs which are heedless of threatened and endangered species, heedless of life-supporting systems necessary for our own survival.

Twenty years ago, I had the privilege of standing beside Archibald MacLeish on the rocky margin of the sea beside his home on the island of Antigua. He was holding in his hand a large conch shell, and, facing the incoming tide, he raised it to his lips—and blew. At first the sound was the softness of the wind. Then it became a muffled voice reaching to great distances. When he lowered the shell, the moment became a listening point at the magical edge of the shoreline.

From The Otter Raft, *No.27, Summer 1982.*

Words of Praise

This tribute to Jim Mattison, trustee and president of Friends of the Sea Otter for many years, was given at the 1994 annual board meeting of Friends of the Sea Otter.

DR. JAMES MATTISON, JR., is a brilliant surgeon for people and a steady guardian for the sea otter who, like a strong, water-worn stone, became my partner in structuring Friends of the Sea Otter in 1968. Thereafter, we were no longer building for the day, but rather for a lasting plan to protect the continuity of the otters.

Following a California State Resource Committee meeting held in San Luis Obispo in 1968, the commercial abalone fishermen were complaining. The red abalone beds, overharvested for many years, were seriously depleted. The men were loudly excited, shouting angry, threatening remarks about the otters. Yes, the otters were the scapegoats, and if ever the southern sea otter needed a friend, it was then. Jim, with his wife, Joanne, and their two sons and one daughter, moved to Salinas in 1958 to join the staff of the Salinas Valley Memorial Hospital. They wanted be closer to Monterey Bay and the ocean shores and what Jim referred to as "the elusive sea otters." Their arrival was a lasting move, and I might add, one that guarded our lasting plan to protect the otters.

Jim immediately set about to photograph "these elusive animals." His inventive mind would have surprised anyone who watched him. It also surprised the sea otters.

First he notified the Monterey Police and California Department of Fish and Game that he was not committing any dastardly act. Then, in the dark of night, Jim and Joanne cautiously boarded a small skiff and rowed out into the bay.

Jim clutched his camera, ready and waiting. Joanne held the turned-off floodlight. Jim scanned the water for the rafting forms of sleeping otters. That great eye-level photograph was about to become reality. The moment came, and Joanne flashed on the powerful light. And the otters, with one quick glance, turned somersaults and disappeared below the surface.

I smile thinking how far and with what speed Jim Mattison has come since that trial expedition when the otters went underwater. Using new equipment, Jim followed the otters with his camera below the surface of the sea and became the first individual to take underwater photographs of the southern sea otter.

By 1971, his excellent photographs accompanied an article in *National Geographic* by Karl Kenyon, the greatest authority on sea otters at that time. Yes, this was the way to open the eyes of the nation. This was news and science as well as beauty. And it was Jim who opened the door for others to follow.

Jim's next achievement, also in 1971, was the film *Back from Extinction*. This educational documentary and accompanying teachers' guidebook targeted schools and educators. It was the first southern sea otter film.

Bill Bryan was next to dive under the water with his camera and emerge with the delightful film *Otters, Clowns of the Sea*. The film presented a delicious scramble of otters rocking and diving in the waters. A joy! Bryan remarked, "Let the otter speak for itself. You don't see anyone wanting to embrace an abalone, do you?"
And again, that crowded year of 1971, Philippe Cousteau arrived in Monterey Bay on the *Calypso* to film *The Unsinkable Sea Otter*. Jud Vandervere, who contributed some footage to the film, introduced Philippe and the crew to what the otters do, and our scientific studies told them how and why they do it. And Jim Mattison was

there to advise and soothe the underwater relationship between man and otters during filming.

That summer, a little otter the crew named Esprit became a close friend of Philippe's. The two—lying on their backs in the water—shared crab meat together. But when the film was finished and the *Calypso* sailed away, Esprit's trust in man caused his death, and his body washed ashore filled with shotgun pellets.

These stories, dear Jim, are only a hint of your sustaining role during the past quarter of a century. You served in so many capacities: from vice president of Friends of the Sea Otter, to carrying out necropsies on illegally shot otters along the Big Sur coast; from trips to Prince William Sound in the '60s, when otters were happily flourishing, to a return to Valdez Bay when thousands of otters lost their lives after the Exxon *Valdez* oil spill. Again, it was at Valdez Bay in the '80s that you volunteered your services to work with the Department of Fish and Game to study the long-lasting effects of the oil spill.

Yes, we're privileged to have had your rugged sense of responsibility toward the otters, and Jim, we want to thank you from the heart.

THE VISION OF FRED FARR

*Adapted from a speech given at a memorial gathering for
Fred Farr on June 15, 1997.*

YES, WE WILL ALL MISS FRED, but he is indelibly imprinted in our
minds and hearts, and will continue, in his visionary way, to guide us
into the future for the Big Sur region. We can't let people drawn to
its immensity and beauty cut the threads of the fabric with little
thought of the consequences.

When Fred became a state senator in 1955, great things began
for nature, and Fred's soft voice became a directive.

As roads were widened and trees were cut, he in turn began to
plant trees. When the California Department of Transportation set
about to "improve" the Big Sur road, blasting the cliffs and canyons
and, to use a line from Robinson Jeffers, "causing rock slides to rattle
and thunder in the throats of living mountains," Fred became
troubled. He turned away from the "freeway category" with a fresh
plan and began to work for California's first scenic highway, and Big
Sur's first scenic road was born.

And during a period when the human race was painfully
indifferent to wildlife, a close neighbor of ours, a mountain lion, was
treed and shot by a young man and his dog. The state and county
rewarded him for this accomplishment with a bounty.

But this lion, which had lived so harmoniously with us, was not
to die in vain. Fred introduced the Bounty Repeal Bill in 1962, and
citizens in due course organized into a strong foundation, and passed

it through six years of moratoriums before finally guarding the life of this beautiful creature by an initiative voted on by the citizens of the entire state.

Down at Big Creek today, in a nature reserve established at the University of California at Santa Cruz through Fred's leadership, three or four mountain lions reside, guarding it as a habitat of their own. They share it harmoniously with people—students, campers and visitors.

And in the nearshore waters of our coast, I'm well aware of the sea otters rafting in kelp beds, cracking urchins and starfish and snails. In 1968, Fred drove his senate committee to Morro Bay, urging me to hop along for the ride. We found a bedlam of commercial abalone fishermen, shouting and blaming the otters for the harvest of what the fishermen called "their resource." Friends of the Sea Otter was born that day.

Yes, thank you, Fred. And may I close with a line from Aldo Leopold?

> The song of the waters is audible to every ear but there is other music in these hills. On a still night, sit quietly and listen. Then you may hear it—a vast pulsing harmony—its notes the lives and deaths of plants, its rhythms spanning the seconds and the centuries.

And Fred Farr, having reached his 86th year, has listened and responded to that harmony.

Sea of Cortez

Black shears slowly
Cut the light
As Frigate drifts through space.
Our craft and bird
Unite in flight
To glide in glittering grace.

A manta ray lifts
A silver shawl
The bird tips wings to arc
And daring slow
It dips and skims
The shadow of the shark.

A luminous void
Unites these forms
An interplay of heart.
Black shears cut space
The stern cuts waves
And neither leaves a mark.

REMEMBRANCES

Lady Bird and the Scenic Road

'THE DAY IN 1966 when Lady Bird Johnson stepped off a plane in Monterey was a day filled with astonishment. She was to be driven down the coast to speak beside Bixby Creek Bridge in Big Sur at the dedication of California's first scenic road.

Before the dedication, a bronze plaque was to be inset and framed in a weathered rock beside the bridge. The rock itself had been waiting beside the road at Grimes Creek some 20 miles south from Bixby. Its shape was not particularly arresting, but the surface was covered with moss and orange and celadon clouds of lichens. Minute ferns and miner's lettuce filled cracks with indented shadows. It was, in short, a stunning background for a plaque.

We set a day for the California Department of Transportation to move the rock up to Bixby Creek. It was not easy to move it all, much less with the care necessary not to hurt the rock's surface. Gordon Newell, our stonemason and sculptor, arrived with the bronze plaque that would be inset in the rock, forever commemorating this moment. The next morning, Lady Bird would arrive. Nat and I drove up to see that everything was in shape, but to our horror the rock and plaque had been vandalized with brilliant purple paint. I let out a scream!

Workmen arrived with a sanding machine and toiled steadily until the First Lady's limousine drew up. The rock was ground to a pure white, and white dust had settled on the ground all around it.

By that time, some 150 people had arrived, but something else seemed to have gone terribly wrong. Lady Bird's bodyguards rushed in on a man with a heavy black cloth over his head and what

142

appeared to be the muzzle of a gun focused in Lady Bird's direction. The guards were quick to jump on the man and pull off the black cloth. It turned out to be Ansel Adams with his camera, trying to photograph the event.

The purple paint that had marred the rock and plaque expressed violent anger at the Vietnam War. Although I, too, was an opponent of that tragic war, the dedication that day related to quite a different kind of battle. Led by Senator Fred Farr, we had fought to defeat the legislative vote to build a four-lane freeway down the Big Sur coast, a construction project that would have blown up the mountains and filled the canyons. In return, we were giving a gift to the people, young and old, knapsack or bicycle, hikers or cars. We were giving these people California's first scenic road.

I was asked to put together some words for Lady Bird to say at the dedication, which happily went off without further interruption:

> I dedicate California's first scenic highway today as the maintenance of a trust—a trust for ourselves and a trust for the generations to follow.
>
> It is a partnership of open space and man's use—a heritage of landscape to be shared by all.
>
> Here on the Monterey coast—this 72 miles of fine shining thread—is a road linking, bridging and weaving the mountain range and the Pacific.
>
> Here, along this road, a value is placed on preserving and strengthening a sense of awe, of wonder.
>
> Here men may seek their release in motion— driving like a flight of birds traveling north and south.
>
> How appropriate that this route has been named "The Cabrillo Highway" after Juan Rodríguez Cabrillo, who sailed past this headland in 1542 with a sense of exploring the unknown—a quest for adventure.

For here, this curve of the road holds a sense of adventure—the adventure of the high view, its majesty and its changing moods.

The people of the nation are indebted to those of you in high office of the State of California and the County of Monterey—indebted to the residents of the coast—who took action to safeguard the land along which this scenic road now travels. For this coastline lies here in the afternoon sun—the western boundary of our continent.

Inscribed on this plaque we can read the words of Robinson Jeffers, from his poem entitled "Continent's End":

> I, gazing at the boundaries of granite and spray
> the established sea-marks, felt behind me
> Mountain and plain, the immense breadth
>   of the continent,
> before me—the mass and doubled stretch of water.

And, at this "continent's end" I stand today and take pride in dedicating this scenic highway for the joy of all who come to share it.

California's first scenic highway was dedicated by Lady Bird Johnson, wife of President Lyndon Johnson, on September 22, 1966.

144

Sharing Nature with George and Gerry Lindsay

Yesterday, I found myself in conversation with my dear friend Dr. George Lindsay, the former director of the California Academy of Sciences in San Francisco. We have both grown older but we still often chuckle together over the most minor of things.

As we talked, George began to tell me about goings-on near his home in Tiburon overlooking the tiny inlets of San Francisco Bay. He described the little tugboat *Mud Hen* as it towed around a barge with a tall arm and clamshell bucket, deepening the channel by scooping up the bottom and dumping it into another barge. Sometimes, he tells me, a bull sea lion charges through the channel in a wash of water, followed by a little harbor seal. All this traffic takes place within a dozen feet of where George's deck chair, with George in it, rests.

George always seems to attract natural events. On one of his visits to our Big Sur home with his wife, Gerry, I told them how worried I was about the golden eagles drawn to our place like a magnet, waiting to sink their talons into my little Yorkie and fly off with her. I could see by George's polite smile that he didn't believe a word of it. As we stepped out onto the porch, my Yorkie tucked herself between our feet like a tiny baby elephant under the huge feet of the herd. Two eagles, perched on a redwood beam eight feet above us, swooped down on the porch, brushing our shoulders with their wings in their attempts to seize my dear Yorkie. I managed to get there first and scoop her safely into my arms.

That same day, after lunch, we drove over to Andrew Molera State Park in Big Sur. It had just rained, and the ground was wet. I carried a measuring tape, since I was studying mountain lions, and knelt to measure several large cougar prints. This led to serious cougar talk as we walked along the park trail toward the pioneer-planted eucalyptus grove. Gerry was thrilled when we discovered several butterfly trees, alive with the flickering of orange-and-black monarch wings or hanging like dried pods, silently waiting for the next step in life. Gerry would later contribute a small jewel of a room to the California Academy of Sciences in memory of her mother, a room filled with butterflies glistening in small spotlights.

Another time when George and Gerry came to see us, a large gray whale was resting directly below our porch. We watched through our binoculars and talked about whales, triggering my memory of a letter George had written to me back in 1967, before we had even met. That year, because of the very small number of gray whales migrating south—only 3,000—some scientists were commencing a scientific "study," and they had a permit to kill 60 whales. Needless to say, George was incensed. I didn't know George then, but somehow he had heard that I often attended board meetings in Washington, D.C., and he wrote to elicit my help. I was horrified after I read his letter. At the Defenders of Wildlife meeting a week later, I decided not to arouse their instant attack on this issue, since the permit had already been granted by the U.S. Fish and Wildlife Service. So, directly after the meeting, I went to the Department of the Interior and asked to see the assistant secretary, Stanley Cain. I had shaken his hand once but did not know him well. He sent out a call for his staff, then led me into a large room with a long, long table. I found myself seated at the end of this table, clutching George's letter, which Cain asked me to read. It was a firm and powerful statement, and I added the gentler comment that they probably hadn't realized what the situation was when they'd granted this permit. Cain listened and asked his staff to look into it. I left the letter with him, and as I rose to leave, many of the staff thanked me.

George never did receive a written response from Cain, which I had assumed he would. But George suddenly heard that the "whale" studyî had been permanently stopped. Although he was distressed to hear that three whales had already been taken, he was elated to know that 57 were saved, possibly including the big whale we stood watching many years later as we reminisced about our first contact.

RECENTLY, I'VE LOOKED FURTHER BACK into George Lindsay's incredible past as a naturalist, only to find a number of inarticulate living creatures bearing his name, including the blind worm snake, *Leptyphlops humulis lindsayi*, found under a rock on the Gulf of California in 1963. There is also a *Scorpion lindsayi*, found in the Cape Sierra of Baja California, as well as a little fly named by Dr. Arnaud for Gerry and George. This little fly is shorter than its name, but once in the literature, George tells me, *Lindsayi* is immortal.

George married Gerry in 1972. A widow with grown children, she volunteered at the California Academy of Sciences and soon became one of a large band of well-trained, enthusiastic volunteers. Filled with fresh ideas for docent work and a wonderful talent for engaging children, she naturally came into contact with the director. It was an excellent marriage, and they gave each other a great deal. She meant the world to George. She loved to come down here to Big Sur, to sit on our porch and hold the world in her hands. She was, alas, fighting cancer yet kept up a steady workload and traveled extensively, including a trip down the Stanislaus River in a rubber raft with the Environmental Defense Fund and visits to our compound at Festina Lente in New Mexico.

The Hopi villages near our *Festina Lente* inspired Gerry to organize trips from the academy. For 40 years my husband, Nat, made a tremendous effort to attend the kachina dances on the Hopi mesa. For decades he collected kachinas and eventually donated them to the Academy for a magnificent Hopi exhibition. Gerry hosted a dinner on opening night for Hopi who had come to the show. During the dinner, one of them, Dr. Emory Sekaquaptewa, got up and began tapping on the table with something wooden, creating the sound of a drum. There, in the dinning room on Washington Street in San Francisco, so far from the Hopi pueblos, we were all suddenly caught up in the rhythm. From down deep in his throat, he began to sing, transporting us to his homeland.

When Gerry died, it was an immense loss to many. George spoke, among others, at the gathering in the great Hall of the Academy. It was not easy to talk about the woman who had meant so much to him. After his few words, he took a letter out of his pocket and read it aloud. It was my last letter to her. She had asked that it be read to her many times.

> Dearest Gerry,
>
> As I drove up the coast this morning, everything was crystal clear with the wind, the kind of wind that pounds the sea. I was thinking of you with your wonderful spirit, and thinking of the places that you have loved and the people who love you. Fallen Leaf, perhaps, in a canoe gliding through the waters in the late afternoon. Pepperwood, with its gentle, rolling slopes which you shared these recent years with George. Big Sur's immensity that enfolds one. And in these moments that are so hard to bear, I hope you can slip into these places and find a peace, knowing that you are a part of them.
>
> Margaret

DR. BETTY DAVIS

The following tribute to Dr. Betty Davis (1921-1981) was written as a memorial to a staunch conservationist who made tremendous contributions to the Friends of the Sea Otter.

DR. BETTY DAVIS served with great distinction as scientific leader and executive secretary of Friends of the Sea Otter. She lived with her husband and family at Hastings Natural History Reservation in Carmel Valley, California. Becoming deeply versed in the southern sea otter's behavior, she was able to advise the Marine Mammal Commission in Washington, D.C. She was an extraordinary person.

Dr. Kenneth Norris called her "a magnificent professional and a wonderful colleague in conservation." He added, "I always thought she leavened what she did with a sense of humor, even a sense of the ridiculous, about some of the things that happen."

For five years, until her death, Betty Davis served as executive secretary for Friends of the Sea Otter. Wonderfully qualified as a scientist for this role that involved issues of wildlife and ecosystems, she moved into our organization with a keen ability to analyze scientific and bureaucratic reports and stand firm with the facts as she saw them.

In the field of science, she earned her B.A. and Ph.D. in zoology at the University of California at Berkeley, specializing in parasitology and protozoology, with honors in her field and Phi Beta Kappa and Sigma Xi memberships. She met her husband, John Davis, at a marine biology class at Hopkins Marine Station, and they were married in 1947. John was to become director of the Hastings Natural History Reservation in 1953, and this became the home for Betty, John and their two children.

Betty soon became immersed in wildlife affairs and in matters impacting wildlife. She took a lead role in the Sierra Club's Wildlife and Endangered Species Committees and served on land and water task forces, as well as on advisory committees to local, state and national government bodies. As principal scientist for Friends of the Sea Otter, her interests fanned out to include the coastal marine habitat in which the otter plays a key role.

"She had a great capacity for drawing others into her orbit and sparking action on the part of the individual who was drawn in," observed Elgin Hurlbert, a retired navy captain long active in Audubon circles. "Actually," he said with a chuckle, "she had a controversial side and an Audubon side."

One side of her personality nurtured those around her, whether it be the small owl blinking from its perch on the fixture over her head in the kitchen, or the young foxes that loved her earlobes. Dr. Ralph Buchsbaum recalls, "Everything she did was absolutely fascinating to her." He goes on to describe a night trip down the coast of Baja California, where Betty leaned over the bow for hours watching the dolphins and the luminescence of the protozoa. Beatrice Howitt, one of her oldest friends, agreed. "She saw remarkable things the rest of us would pass over."

When John was on his sabbatical, studying the rufus-collared sparrow in Lima, Peru, his family went with him, and Betty established a home there which many biologists from museums in the north called their "oasis." She brought along her microscope and immediately focused the glass on the drinking water. In the first drop, she discovered protozoans moving about unlike any she had ever seen. "Wow, look at this one!" she was to exclaim again and again. In ornithological terms, it was like a birder discovering a lifer. Dr. Oliver Pearson, now a professor emeritus of zoology at U.C. Berkeley, visited Betty and John—and he was quick to tell us that Betty boiled the water thoroughly after these discoveries and kept her visiting scientists healthy and well fed. "Betty herself was an oasis," he added.

Back on the Monterey Peninsula, whether it was fighting off the threat of supertankers or writing long reports supporting the otter's role in the ecology, she was ever involved in skirmishes, setting the course of action which Friends of the Sea Otter continues to follow.

Jo Stallard, president of the local Audubon Society, summed it up when she said, "We have touched her in different periods of time and in different ways and are all changed by the touching." When I telephoned John Twiss, the executive director of the Marine Mammal Commission in Washington, D.C., to tell him of Betty's death, there was a silence. Then he said, "So rare; she was so rare." As a scientist she was completely unique in our country today.

DARK SHADOWS

Rhythm of the Birds

"I like to feel this rhythm;
I like to feel we are not superior to other forms of creation,
but co-equal with them, each in his own sphere."

—Robert Gibbings

THE RHYTHM OF BIRDS—and their perfect coordination in flight when a flock, as one entity, suddenly wheels and curves over itself like a veil in the wind. We watch this happen with awe and wonder, since we have nothing similar in our own instincts. We know not what they can do, nor how or why they do it. We can only revel in their beauty.

But with the sea otters, our instincts share a closer association. Our observations tell us what they do, and our scientific studies tell us how and why they do it. It has been an intense period of learning as the otters rock and tumble in the swells, holding their pups on their chests, introducing their young to that particular rhythm of their habitat in the sea. As they cluster and disappear, we find them curious, humorous and feisty, as well as trusting and loving—and these qualities bring us intuitively into a relationship with the otters. Thus, our growing knowledge engenders growing concern.

It was the loss of over 17,000 seabirds in a single summer in 1981 that first aroused public concern over the use of gill and trammel nets in Monterey Bay. In the summer of 1982, our fear that sea otters were also falling victim to the nets proved true. In the summer of 1984, the state legislature finally banned the large mesh nets from within the 15-fathom depth curve in Monterey Bay—yet in the central and southern portions of their range, the otters continued to drown. As state senator Ken Maddy stepped forward to introduce legislation to extend the prohibition of the large mesh nets throughout the shallow waters of the rest of the otter range, newly confirmed Department of Fish and Game director Jack Parnell enacted an emergency net closure to prevent any additional otter drownings until the bill become law.

Now we are able to focus again on the other dark shadows threatening storms up and down the coast: the Department of the Interior's unveiling of its new Five-Year Offshore Oil and Gas Leasing Program, which will target three lease sales within the next five-year time period along the sea otter range and the Big Sur coast and the continuing menace of a tanker spill as tankers lose power and drift toward shore or, as we have seen off San Francisco, split in half, still seeping oil from their sunken wreckages six months later.

Together, we must face these dark shadows. Together, we must preserve the rhythm.

From The Otter Raft, *No. 33, Summer 1985.*

The Fabric of Existence
Weaves Itself Whole

Adapted from a presentation to the Endangered Species Symposium, Washington, D.C., June 12, 1974.

A FEW WEEKS AGO we sailed up the inland passage from Vancouver and crossed the turbulent waters of Hecate Strait to the Queen Charlotte Islands—clustered landforms intricately channeled apart. With their wild waters and deep woods they are referred to today as "The Islands of Cedar and Salmon." But a hundred years ago this region drew the trader and the sea hunter from around the world for the rich, dark fur of the sea otter. Along these shores the sea otter was abundant and for the taking.

The Haida villages we visited in the Queen Charlottes are only myth and legend today. Their totem poles which we found in desolate loneliness on Anthony Island are symbols of a culture in which the entire environment became an art form. But just as the sea otter was slaughtered for his fur, exploited to the point of extermination, this society, too, was destroyed.

Survivors of Vitus Bering's last voyage in 1741 collected the first sea otter pelts for the market. For the next 100 years, fur traders invaded every island in the North Pacific, offering iron tools, nails, pots, and buttons for the skin of the sea otter. In 1785, George Dixon, aboard a British ship, sailing from Boston, brought home 6,000 skins. Along with much bloodshed, these traders left smallpox, measles, and other diseases in their wake.

During the ugly slaughter of the sea otter in the north, plunder commenced to the south, including the coast of California down to Baja. Padres from the Spanish missions and also Russians with enslaved Aleuts stripped the Pacific waters of otter herds. (Aleuts were said to have killed 800 otters during one week in San Francisco Bay.) By 1911, an International Fur Seal Treaty halted further exploitation. At that time, it was believed that no sea otters were left alive.

But along the California coast today we have what we consider to be a valiant return—out of small gene pools, out of fragile remnants—the rebuilding of a population of sea otters.

It was in 1938 when a herd of some 300 sea otters was observed at Bixby Landing along the Monterey coast. This was the first large herd reported since 1831 and, as the *San Jose Mercury Herald* noted, "Their appearance brought scientists as near to wild rejoicing as men of their profession are permitted." Dr. Harold Heath, connected with Hopkins Marine Laboratory, identified the species as *Enhydra lutris nereis* or the southern sea otter. And it is these sea otters—remnants of that once great population that I will now show you in action so that you can enjoy their charm and meet them as friends.

Let me share with you images of wild otters in action—of unlimited freedom in action—something rare and sadly missing from the human experience today:

> Diving, feeding, vigorously playing, the sea otter swims, belly-up, propelled by webbed hind feet, effortlessly moving in the endless violence and constant rhythm of the sea.
>
> Large beds of kelp are common throughout the otter's range in California and offer protected areas for resting. Otters often raft in clusters among the kelp fronds.
>
> Population growth of the sea otter is naturally slow due, in part, to the fact that each mature female bears

only one young every two years, a condition which permits long and solicitous care of each pup. The pup lies motionless on its mother's chest while she licks and grooms it. It is carried about and left to float while she dives for food. From the beginning, the pup is buoyant like a small floating balloon. It attempts to dive after its mother but cannot keep both ends of its body under the water at once. Here, it tries and fails.

The otter is unique among marine mammals in having no subcutaneous fat. It relies on a blanket of air trapped among the fibers of its fur for insulation against the cold, as well as for buoyancy. In the event of an oil spill, damage to the otter's fur would be fatal by depriving him of the warmth and buoyancy essential to his existence.

It is young males who leave the familiar herd; it is they who venture forth. They scatter and regroup in what appears to be new communities at the farthest edge of the range.

Underwater, the sea otter has a flowing grace in motion. He explores with his forepaws and navigates with his webbed hind feet. His preferred foods are sea urchins, abalone, crabs and mussels. Observers have recorded some 30 different food items that he eats. Since urchins feed on the rootlike structures of kelp, and kelp beds nurture and protect fish populations as well as sift particles of nutrients down to abalone, the otter's role in controlling urchins is part of a food chain and provides an example of the balance of nature at work.

The sea otter is unique among marine mammals in its use of tools—usually rocks. Returning from a dive with a rock carried in the loose fold of skin under one

armpit, he lies on his back, places the rock on his chest
and uses his nimble forepaws to break open the shells.

Perhaps the killing of a hundred thousand sea otters during a
century and a half of slaughter resulted in the illusion of a stable
super-abundance of abalone and other shellfish along the California
coast. The otters have occupied these waters for thousands of years
and it is clear that an ecological balance must have existed among
the otters, the abalone, urchins, crabs and clams, as well as the
coastal Indians.

With the otter's disappearance, a cumulative backlog of shellfish
built up and, when commercial exploitation of abalone commenced,
this industry was harvesting a field unnaturally abundant with abalone
untouched by otters and almost untouched by man for some 40 years.
In the Monterey area, they landed in excess of 41 million pounds
before the beds were depleted and the industry moved south to
Morro Bay. This was a time when the sea otter herd had not yet been
sighted. At Morro Bay, the industry commenced yearly landings
higher than any ever recorded. As the harvest peaked—and began at
once to decline—the sea otters (now recognized and building up their
herds along the coast) were eating the remnants of abalone left by the
industry along the Monterey coastal area. These sea otters began to
move south toward Morro Bay just in time to be blamed for the
drastic decline in shellfish; just in time to be blamed for the over-
harvest of abalone; and just in time to be called a "predator in
competition with man."

It's perfectly true that the sea otter likes to eat abalone. However,
procuring one is no easy task. Using a stone tool, he must hammer
the abalone to free it from the rock to which it clings. Observers have
watched the otter make as many as six dives to obtain this big snail.

But why, we might ask, is the abalone resource declining along
the entire California coast, much of which is far from the otter's
range? The California Department of Fish and Game repeatedly
states that "there can be little or no human harvest of invertebrates

within the range of the sea otter." And then one wonders if the Indians, otters and abalone were ever a balanced community when the sea otter was so abundant. It is interesting to note that the Indian middens along the Monterey coast show that these people relied heavily on abalone for food and, although they were competing with abundant numbers of otters, the Indians were still able to gather plentiful amounts of this shellfish. Don Howard, an archeologist studying the Carmel Indian middens, has found quantities of red and black mature abalone along with whale-rib wedges used to pry abalone from underwater rocks. Many of these shells show these wedge scars on their margins.

So it would appear that in the past Indian, otter and abalone were in balance. But today, with human population soaring, skin diving increasing some 430 percent in the last decade, abalone selling for $5.90 a pound, and the sea otter population precariously low, this balance has been destroyed. Lawful taking of abalone has failed even to maintain a sustained yield.

Today, the California Department of Fish and Game would have us believe, by their frequent reports in the press, that there is literally a "population explosion" among the otters whose numbers they estimate to be as high as between 1,600 and 1,800 when in fact, we know the aerial head counts of December 1973 and March 1974 were 941 and 953 respectively. By their own admission, the Department of Fish and Game extrapolated their figures to include possibly unseen otters. What they fail to emphasize is that two years earlier, 1,060 otters were counted in an aerial survey which suggests that the otter population has lessened and that the Department of Fish and Game's "population explosion" is a figure of speech emerging from unseen otters.

But whatever the estimates, our organization, Friends of the Sea Otter, considers the California sea otter population to be small and, by any rational standard, extremely precarious.

Why does the department take the stand it does? It can only be because they are keyed to commercial and sport use of resources, and the otter is not a resource useful to them. After reading "The Report on the California Sea Otter" (following a five-year study by department invertebrate biologists) we have learned little about the social structure of the otter herds, their pattern of movements, their sexual reproduction, their threats from marine pollution. Instead, we have read about "Invertebrate Resources (used by man) Being Depleted by Foraging Activities of the Otter." One might, of course, look at other factors causing depredation.

Still clear in the memory of some of the "old-timers" at Pismo Beach is one particular minus tide morning when 150,000 persons were recorded digging what may have amounted to 1,000,000 clams. "They came with forks, spears, shovels and swords," wrote the *Five Cities Press Recorder*. Volunteer firemen from three cities came to patrol the beach with first-aid equipment and resuscitators. At least 40 clammers suffered puncture wounds; three people drowned; one had a coronary; uncounted children were lost; and wardens, checking licenses and limit-counts, gave up. Naturally, that was an exceptional day, for the next low tide only brought a count of 60,000 people!

On the July 4th weekend of 1979, the Pismo State Beach staff, in their own words, "survived once again four days of mass madness"— 4,500 motor homes, travel trailers and tents bordered the high tide line and 9,000 dune buggies, motorcycles and four-wheel drive vehicles swarmed over the campsites. A total of 163,000 visitors and 78,000 vehicles were counted and 13,700 gallons of sewage and 450-cubic-yards of trash were carted away after the weekend subsided. But the best minus tides for clamming come in winter, when the water is reduced in depth to 1.6 (and 1.9 every seven years). "Clammers," the chief ranger explained to me, "are not experienced people. For example, in 1975, 19 people lost their lives just digging for clams here at Pismo Beach." He went on to say that an average of 5,000 clammers could be found any time at low tides or holidays. The Fish and Game warden estimated that approximately 30,000 clams would be taken on those days. With human competition, a clammer—permitted 10 clams—is fortunate to take home six. At Pismo Beach, five miles are open to clamming the year round, but one mile with the heaviest human activity has been closed since March 1, 1976. No big clams remain there, but thousands of baby clams are in the sand. "The plan is to let the babies grow before turning the clammers loose on them once again," said the chief ranger.

"Tell me," I asked, "do the otters have a chance at any of these clams along the beach?" He laughed, then confessed that he hadn't seen a single otter in the waters off Pismo Beach. "But," he added, "some reliable sources had reported seeing one or two otters during the year."

To keep the otters from advancing to Pismo Beach for clams, to keep the otters from settling in Morro Bay for abalone, to keep the otters from moving north to San Francisco's declining market-crab resource, the California Department of Fish and Game will be recommending to the Marine Mammal Commission a program to restrict the range of the California sea otter and to control its population.

How does Fish and Game propose to have this carried out? Although their plans are not finalized, statements made by their invertebrate biologists advocate restriction of otters within a limited range (approximately their present refuge, with modifications) and the capturing of all otters which stray outside this prescribed area. They have proposed placing these otters in aquariums around the world. They have opposed translocation of otters to any region of the California coast. They have even discussed the methods of 'cropping' otters and have considered birth-control implants in female otters.

In examining these measures under discussion, we must realize that, at the present time, an estimated 200 otters are outside their refuge. This refuge, established by the state legislature in 1941, was enlarged in 1959 to further protect otters, not to limit their movements to a prescribed area.

If sea otters are translocated back into this refuge, it will not only mean a continual operation against the natural fluctuations of otter herds, it will bring about overcrowding of the refuge and could mean starvation. If the department is relying in their own statements that "otters have depleted their refuge," this present proposal is simply a death sentence.

By opposing translocation to any other region of the state, Fish and Game leaves the otters exposed to threats of extinction by a major oil spill.

The proposal to capture otters for transplant to aquariums around the world is fraught with obstructions because of the high mortality during transport, the difficulty of maintenance in captivity, the high cost of feeding, and the need for quiet and privacy for healthy living which is contrary to public facilities designed to display animals for crowds. In addition, sea otter births in captivity have repeatedly failed. No pup has survived.

The proposal to crop sea otters or to experiment with artificial means to impede reproduction, is unthinkable and is contrary to every conservation-minded aim among thinking people.

Furthermore, added to the threat of oil spills that hangs precariously over the herds, the life of the sea otter is in jeopardy from recreational crafts and fishermen's boats whose propellers have lacerated and killed a growing number of these animals. High levels of cadmium found in the tissues of others may be producing systematic problems. DDT, DDE, and PCBs in the marine organisms fed on by otters could have harmful effects on these mammals.

The bodies of 50 or more otters have been washed ashore, carrying gunshot wounds or knife scars. Abalone fishermen wage a continual war on the otters but their violent actions often escape notice in coastal fogs. Forty or 50 otter bodies are packed in the department's freezer. They have not yet been necropsied for the cause of death.

Friends of the Sea Otter favors an unrestricted range for the otter along the California coast. Studies by Dr. John Pearse have shown that the otter enhances marine life by increasing the diversity of plant and animal forms. Although we would prefer that he move naturally along the coast, due to these present threats we favor establishing a secondary refuge. San Nicolas Island, the outermost Channel Island off the Santa Barbara coast, is one Exposed to heavy seas and not frequented by small craft, it is protected from serious oil spills and human pollutants. Guadalupe Island, off the coast of Mexico, is another consideration. Here, the Guadalupe fur seal was brought back from near extinction, to re-establish itself.

In addition, we urge that mariculture (shellfish nurseries) which is now in the beginning stages of development, be strengthened by federal funding so that abalone (like oysters) can be farmed and the controversy resolved between abalone fisheries and otter conservationists.

May I close with emphasis on the positive measures already enacted to guard the sea otter? Through federal action, it is "a fully protected mammal." Through state legislation, it has a refuge. The Endangered Species Act of 1973 provides protection for "isolated and unique" populations. The federal Marine Mammal Commission has a guardian jurisdiction over the sea otter.

It is to this commission that we look for a judgment that could not otherwise become disentangled from the local market-catch of shellfish, from the mobs of people digging clams, and from the increase in popularity of skin diving.

No one expects the California sea otter to repopulate his former range in large numbers—but the future of approximately 1,000 otters hangs in the balance today. His return from near extinction places him as a symbol of hope for all American wildlife. Let us hold to this hope for, as Charles Ives observed, "The fabric of existence weaves itself whole."

Is Solitude an Empty Hope?

Adapted from a presentation to the Governor's Conference on California Beauty, Panel on Parks and Greenbelts, Los Angeles, 1968.

ON A SUMMER'S DAY ALONG THE MONTEREY COAST, the cars form long, patient lines to enter Pfeiffer Big Sur State Park. From day to day, I watch these lines and am repeatedly reminded of the words of John Muir—"They come like thirsty sponges to imbibe."

Yes, our people come, cars filled with children, willingly traveling great distances to enjoy camping under shadowed redwoods and sycamore beside a rushing river. Our parks have become a destination type recreation in which man seeks his release in motion and carries his family with him. Walt Whitman wrote:

> I take the open road,
> Healthy, free, the world before me.
> The long brown path before me
> leading wherever I choose.

Today, "the long brown path" is four lanes of asphalt,—but the choice is still ours' —and our California Parks, with their diversity of landscape, are becoming more and more the destination of this choice.

Motion is an outlet from the conformity of everyday life, an escape from frustrations, from barriers. But, we might ask, is this escape a renewal of inner contentment? More and more, the machine exacts from man the grim price of adaptation and adaptation is the road back to conformity.

Still,—our average man is free to choose.

He may take his family to Doheny Beach State Park—to join cars drawn up in masses of glittering metal—no privacy but elbow room, no space but the sky above. Or, Lake Elsinor State Park, —a different selection , where the roar of motor boats may quickly quickens the heart. Or, perhaps, instead, this man will choose a trip to Point Lobos Reserve—superbly beautiful, fragile and small, where seagardens and Cypress grow undisturbed, and kelp and sea otter are rocked by the ebb and flow of tides.

But the size of this reserve and the delicacy of its ecology are not suited to mass use or—mass recreation. In short, it cannot be used—it can only be experienced. For here we find a sanctuary, a place to observe the mysteries. Point Lobos is a quality reserve for scenic enjoyment and scientific study—a storehouse of treasure for today,—and for the future. Yet, out of the 183 units in the state park system, only 15 are so designated. Why have we not preserved more?

But these 183 units offer the public a broad selection of choices, —graced as we are by this beautiful land over which swift travel is gradually making places merge. Yes, places are merging and the *sense of place* is vanishing, with strip developments interlacing each city and town.

It may well be that our parks will become the last areas to retain this sense of place—an individuality preserved through respect for the natural landscape and open space.

Yet we must be on guard, or parks will be pressed by the oversweeping population into over-development and scarred by overuse. A wood path, carpeted with moss, will be paved with asphalt. Ancient trees will be cleared as hazards. The multi-patterned ground cover will become pulverized like the Masai reserves in East Africa (only here by human feet rather than the feet of cattle herds), devoid of wildlife and sprayed for insects, silent of bird-song, and the tent-to-tent camping will become another suburbia, vacant of any sense but that of the crowd. How can man, in the future, be rescued from the crowd?

Is solitude an empty hope?

As a member of the state park commission, I have recently been involved in a selection of parks to be acquired through the 1964 bond issue funds. These acquisitions were aimed primarily to alleviate crowding.

This selection was not, I was to discover, the weighing of one fine landscape against another, one rushing trout stream against a free, unplanted hill. For we were dealing with quantitative as well as qualitative criteria.

Where, we were asked, could the greatest benefits serve the greatest number of people for the amount of money spent? Many factors question the validity of this criterion. As David Brower of the Sierra Club reminds us, "If you follow the precept of the greatest good to the greatest number of people, the greatest number can wipe out the greatest good." Geographical distribution, as well as specialized recreational demands, was given careful consideration. Adequate and practical locations for picnic tables, campsites and parking lots were keenly the foremost factors, keenly examined.

Two years ago, over 1.5 million campers were turned away in state parks due to lack of facilities. Here, we are dealing with clear-cut numerical needs, a mathematical equation that the computer handles very well.

But what of the qualitative criteria? Far more subtle, far less defined, here we handle ideas veiled in shadow. Quality has philosophic overtones. Quality's emphasis is not on the hot showers, not the place near at hand to have the car lubricated and buy groceries—not necessarily on the conveniences.

How can we place a value on quality?

"How much is a walk through a beautiful park?" asked Hugo Fisher. In answer, a computer might tie in the economics of the area or place with the dollar sign on the distance a man drives to reach the experience.

But what is the value placed on preserving and strengthening the sense of awe, of wonder? How can we credit the value of a web of peace and beauty—something beyond the boundaries of human existence?

And for children, how important are memories built up in an afternoon on a granite slope in the Sierra where the only sound is the Clark's nutcracker and the only scent, the bough of a juniper? This is the way a child learns to be receptive to what lies around him. How valuable is the sense of wonder?

What is the experience of a redwood grove—a self-contained world, apart from the crowd, a place to listen?

How do we place a value on silence?

Here in America, our tastes are still unripe. Is it that we have not lived long enough on this continent to grow close to the earth and make it a part of our dreams? Shouldn't we turn to our parks, and by the very character of their planning and handling, assign them a top priority for training a stronger sense of appreciation—of taste?

Let's shift the preoccupation with artifice and ease to one of adventure in the natural landscape, an adventure in which each individual works for his pleasure. In developing parks, let's not allow the slowest to set the pace. Instead, let's set the quality of experience high and hard to reach, making it a challenge and an accomplishment. Let us draw the public out of their cars for a walk, for a hike, for a pack-sack trip, for a fishing trip on a mountain stream, for a high view.

The softness in our public is truly a challenge for park planners. Let's make our people strong! For, in the words of Rachel Carson: "Those who contemplate the beauty of earth find reserves of strength that will endure as long as life lasts."

THE CALIFORNIA DILEMMA

Adapted from a presentation to the National Audubon Convention,
Sacramento, California, November 14, 1966

HOW MANY OF YOU, with natural grace, trace the years of your life
along the outlines of an imperishable landscape—a landscape
representing a fundamental structure in your life, a place to return to,
a continuity which offers stability and strength?

> A bend of a great river. . .
> A promontory, encircled by the sea
> The etched silhouette of peaks. . . .
> The dry, sharp shadows of the canyon-lands. . . .
> An imperishable forest of trees.

My husband and I visited such a forest this fall in the slender valleys
of Mount Olympus in the Olympic National Park in the Pacific
Northwest: the Hoh, the Quinault, the Queets and the Bogacheil,
valleys of rich tapestry under a perpetual fall of moisture, with giant
columns of Sitka spruce, hemlock, Douglas-fir, and red cedar
reaching up through red alders and the floating shapes of big-leaf
maple, reaching up well over 200 feet as great living monuments to
the present. And, one momentous day, when the span of a life cycle
comes to a close, a giant will come crashing down, to stretch out
horizontally as a monument to the past on which young seedlings will
take root and find nourishment. Thus, the future growth takes root in

the past, and here we find a strength, for here is a form of immortality through continuity.

Camping in the Bogacheil Valley, we found ourselves in an early cathedral. It was scale, shape, light and shadow—with a silence placed on every bough.

Yet the morning we returned along the trail, some two miles before we reached the outside park boundary, we heard a sudden new sound, a warning of the world outside—the nasal screaming of the mechanical saw on adjacent national forest land. Both immortality and continuity were interrupted by a forward march of "progress."

Under commercial pressures repeatedly leveled at this national park, we might well ask the question: Are we assured that this park sanctuary is imperishable?

In the adjoining national forest, an inviting and beautifully planned trail leads to a magnificent grove of trees in front of which a sign has been placed. It reads:

> This is probably the most heavily forested acre of timber in the Pacific Northwest. 390,000 board feet of lumber would build over 40 large ranch-style homes today. The Douglas-fir are 375 years old and average 285 feet in height. The hemlock are 150 years old and average 150 feet in height. Since first measured in 1956, the stand has increased to 396,000 board feet, nearly enough for another home.

Can man's expression of the aesthetic in these 40 ranch-style homes, whose span of use is perhaps 40 years, compete with the aesthetic experienced by man in this grove, where the life span, if uninterrupted, is perpetuity?

Is this a form of progress? "The simple faith in progress," wrote Norbert Weiner, "is not a conviction belonging to strength, but one belonging to acquiescence—and hence, weakness."

In Jedediah Smith Redwoods State Park on the California north coast, a "National Tribute Grove" was established in 1947— "A living memorial to the dead of World War II." Funds were raised by some 4,000 donors, including the Garden Clubs of America, the Daughters of the American Revolution and the Save-the-Redwoods League. These funds were matched by the state of California for what was described as "a fitting and imperishable tribute."

Yet the California state highway department, relying on what it calls the "user benefit ratio," felt obliged to route a highway that would remove 80 acres of prime redwoods out of a 140-acre parcel of this park. This route would pass through the summit of the terrain with a cut 120 feet deep and 700 feet wide. The scale of this cut would not only destroy the aesthetic, dwarfing the trees, but would destroy what we might call the portal opening into the inner chamber. It would destroy the sequence of the native environment, the life zone, with its water storage, its light and shadow. Windrow and sun-scald would gradually reach in and remove the bordering forest.

With the destruction of another redwood forest, a state-owned park, the human social system tragically suffers another poverty. Is public parkland, may I ask, a freedom, or is it a discipline?

This controversy between parks and highways is a strange one. Both work to benefit the citizen; both belong to the citizen; each discharges an invitation for citizen use—for citizen pleasure. This close interrelation between highways and parks poses a curious question. Is it not odd that a program for highways—constructing, broadening or straightening a route—sometimes demands the price of a forest, a park or a scenic area it is intended to service?

A state's custody of parks, condoning a breach of trust by another state agency, might suggest that a public security was being undermined. State parks are entrusted properties, and the state park commission shoulders this trust—yet is powerless to safeguard it while the division of highways retains the right to bisect these lands with massive highways.

After years of debate, this issue was improved upon at Prairie Creek Redwoods State Park, with a ridge route planned to bypass park boundaries. It is still unresolved at Jedediah Smith Redwoods State Park, though Governor Brown requested that the division of highways halt action until a bypass route can be studied in depth. It is still unresolved at Emerald Bay on Lake Tahoe. If all the bypasses requested by the state division of parks to protect superlative areas were strung together in one line, they would total no more than 15 miles—15 miles out of 3,492 miles of multilane highways and freeways in the state.

"Where there is no vision"—to quote the Bible— "the people perish."

As David Medd noted, the Native American passed through the land with caution and respect, "like a fish through water." Today, we often cross our magnificent Sierra over erosive scars cut through granite mountains, leveling the road for parking turnouts and signs.

What is gained? We are opening up the country for the mass of people with an entrance of ease. Does this entrance of ease mean progress? What is lost? The conformity of concrete robs the challenge, robs the accomplishment, robs the adventure and destroys an aesthetic.

In developing our state parks for popular recreational use, we are serving the owners of the land—the public. These parks are being used. But what does this word "use" mean? Does the word "use" override the word "preserve"? Will wildlife, for example, become a commodity for use, just as trees might be used, if we were to open up our parks to the lumbermen?

As Freya Stark pondered, "can beauty walk along the edge of opposites?"

The California division of parks has been under fire for years for its slow development program. But the facts are simple—the largest percentage of the park budget has been funneled into the fastest vanishing commodity—land. Yet our governor-elect, Ronald Reagan, suggested during his campaign "that an inventory of parklands be made to determine what is not now being used." "For this land," he said, "ought to be put on the market and sold."

Those of us working with parks knew better—for land that is idle now is no reason for alarm, it is reason for rejoicing! It gives us a land bank.

During the coming decade, our principal funds will be channeled into park development. Attendance at state parks last year was 35 million, with well over 1.5 million campers turned away due to lack of facilities. The budget for development alone during the next five years is approximately $25 million a year.

Standing beside a concession administrator in Yosemite Valley this summer, I gazed with fascination at the network of tent-living under the trees on the valley floor.

"They figure," my companion explained, "that if one studies this maze with enough care, a person can cut just one rope and the total tent community will fall flat on the ground."

How will the crowd be rescued from the crowd? Is solitude an empty hope?

Safety measures are tightening in our parks. Safety is gradually covering the heavily used trails with asphalt. It inserts railings and warning signs at the climax of the excursion. Safety clears out underbrush, the habitat for birds and wildlife, as a fire hazard. It cuts great limbs off giant trees for the protection of the visitor below—also a cautious measure to avoid lawsuits. Safety can spray the air for insects and empty it of birdsong. Safety stirs neurotically under the possible threat of bubonic plague—and dispatches ground squirrels with 1080 poison. It looks at skunk and fox with fear of rabies. It kills coyote with a cyanide gun, calling him "predator," though his prey is often the very animals being eliminated by man as a "hazard." And the deer, said to be overgrazing the park—is a hunting season proposed? And what of the mountain lion who preys on the deer?

In the words of Lois Crisler, living as she did with the wolves and caribou in Alaska, "If you refuse danger too much, you refuse life."

As a member of the California state park commission, I have recently been involved in a selection of parks to be acquired through the 1964 bond issue funds of $150 million.

This selection, I was to discover, was not the weighing of one fine landscape against another—one wildlife swamp against a silent forest. For we were dealing with quantitative as well as qualitative criteria. A method was set up, using the computer, "to insure maximum return on investment without violation of qualitative standards."

Where, we were asked, could the greatest benefits serve the greatest number of people for the money spent? In brief, much of the problem of analysis and recommendation was thrown on the machine. "Yes, the greatest weakness of the machine," wrote Norbert Weiner, "is that it cannot take into account the vast range of probability that characterizes the human situation."

In short, the greatest number of people served soon became the governing factor.

But how difficult it was to place a computer number on the qualitative experience! How much is a walk through a redwood forest? What is the value of a lagoon filled with migratory birds? Is there a price on the mysteries of life? Will we, someday, place a dollar sign on silence?

In Orange County in Southern California, the state purchased 39 acres of flat land adjoining Bolsa Chica State Beach and a freeway. It was high on the computer priority list, for though it cost approximately $4 million, it would benefit the people by parking 4,000 cars.

On the other side of the ledger, with an emphasis on the qualitative standards, Sugar Pine Point on Lake Tahoe was a $9 million purchase, adding some 2,000 acres to the state park system. These 2,000 acres contained a quality in scenery and trees—ponderosa pine, incense cedar, juniper and lodgepole pine—a quality in beauty stretching from the blue waters of Lake Tahoe up through rising land, and a full-water stream pouring down from protecting ridges.

Here, this Tahoe park destination, if handled with care, can offer both scenery and recreational use in a compatible manner.

California, one might say, is lavishly endowed with a varied choice of landscapes—and the park system contains 1,961 units.

On a trip to Point Lobos State Reserve, where kelp and sea otters are rocked by tides. But the limited size of this reserve and the delicacy of its ecology are not suited to mass use, mass recreation. Yes, it can be experienced and appreciated—but not "used"—for here we find a sanctuary which leaves a lasting impression on its visitors.

Alas, this reserve is still subject to threats. Last year the proposed installation of an oil refinery, north of Point Lobos, presented the possibilities of injurious effects on marine life from shore currents carrying oil spillage from the loading of tankers. The human element of error is present, regardless of regulations to avoid spillage. One quick accident and the tide pools would be contaminated, pelagic birds unable to rise above the oiled water and herds of sea otters lost—not to mention the recreational use of the white sands of some 10 state-owned beaches destroyed within the radius of pollution.

But the Army Corps of Engineers, which had to give official permission, was introduced to the sea otters, which in turn were on the endangered species list, thus halting the permission to sanction supertankers to enter Monterey Bay.

On September 21 of 1966, a small, attractive, openhearted woman stood at Bixby Creek Bridge, some 15 miles south of Point Lobos. She stood beside a rock in which a bronze plaque had just been set. It was a clear, clean day filled with color and restless motion in the sea below.

It was Mrs. Lyndon Johnson, there to dedicate California's first scenic highway as the "maintenance of a trust, a trust for ourselves and a trust for the generations to follow."

This 72 miles of coast road, from Carmel south to the Monterey County line, only a generation ago was Walt Whitman's "long brown path." Only an upper and a lower coastal trail led from Big Sur to the isolated ranches down the coast.

In the early '30s came the road, narrow and winding—and with the road came a few settlers. Twenty years passed before pressures commenced to "modernize" this coastal route. It was designated by the state legislature as "a future freeway," which meant blasting the precipitous mountains, filling the redwood canyons and leaving scars of construction never to heal. Residents in the area rose up in one body and pronounced disaster.

Due to this local opposition and the leadership of state senator Fred Farr, the coast highway was removed from the state freeway system. Unguided real-estate developers were spreading down the coast, since no zoning would permit close-knit houses between the road and the sea. In addition, increasing tourist traffic could instigate a string of restaurants, motels and gas stations.

Since the division of highways was correct in claiming that the present road could not handle these proposed developments, a group of citizens, with county cooperation, set about to control the potential developments by a land use program defined in a master plan. The plan pressed the concept of preserving open space without imposing unjustifiable restrictions on the landowners now and in the future.

It was two and a half years before the plan was accepted, for many people had viewed it as freedom at stake. Gradually, they became accustomed to thinking in a new way. A truth came through. They saw that a disciplined freedom had been placed on the land, and out of this discipline came the first prospectus of a scenic highway. This scenic highway, with its corridor, could be defined as a partnership of open space and man's use.

For "we travel together," said Adlai Stevenson in his last speech, "passengers on a little spaceship, dependent on its vulnerable supplies of air and soil, committed for our safety to its security and peace, preserved from annihilation only by the careful work and, I will say, the love we give our frail craft."

THE OTTER'S SECOND CHANCE

Adapted from the epilogue in Roy Nickerson's
The Sea Otter, *Chronicle Books, 1994.*

Low tide—and the sea lies like pewter with a polish of silver from the slant of the morning sun. Heavy brine, that life-giving support, slides out and slips back under the massive canopy of kelp, carrying a momentum that rolls pebbles onto intimate beaches only to draw them back to the underwater world with a scrunching sound.

But now one perceives another subtlety through the magnified clarity of the water—the flowing grace in motion of a sea otter, a southern sea otter, exploring with its forepaws and navigating with its webbed hind feet. And now, another otter bursts through the pattern of kelp, whiskers fanning out as it parts the fronds while holding between its forepaws a clutch of mussels ripped from nearshore rocks below the surface.

The privilege of watching this smallest of marine mammals from the shore offers each of us a personal reunion with life in the sea. Gradually, as we familiarize ourselves with the little otter, the whole ecology of the coast commences to unfold. An empathy is exchanged between us as the sea otter plays and splashes, alertly raising its head to focus upon us with curiosity before it turns with a flip and somersaults beneath the surface. This vitality draws people to the edge of the sea, its sands, its promontories, as well as its underwater world in which the otter pursues a key role.

But, oh, the helpless innocence of this animal—but yet its undeniable strength, its valiant return from near extinction! Following the holocaust of the fur trade, when herds were scattered and slaughtered, the once unlimited freedom for these playful animals in the lap and slap of the sea appeared totally gone.

Today, this remnant population is part of the total picture of our over-strained marine environment—over-strained not by otters but by increasing and cumulative human pressure or, may I say, human greed. "The sense of continuing creation," wrote Rachel Carson, "the relentless drive of life."

Yes, it's the sea otter's second chance!

How can we ensure the southern sea otter a continuity of life? Will it always be competing with man? How can we protect the otter from offshore oil spills? Is it a vassal to man, with man's management and man's manipulations limiting its freedom? Can it survive?

These are the questions in 1968 that sparked the initiative to found Friends of the Sea Otter—with a dictate to stand firmly behind a sound conservation program for this unique sea mammal. As the meaning of their rarity became clearer, it awakened the public's response. Threats and jeopardies to its welfare became more exposed. Actions by the abalone industry, as well as fatal violations of the otter's protected status, reinforced the realization that this little mammal truly needed a friend.

For the abalone fishermen did not regard the sea otters as "a rarity back from extinction"—but as a predator in competition with man! Immense shell mounds were piled like dikes or berms, leaving their own silent story of man's relation to these shellfish—indicating excessive predation.

There was no room for the otter!

ETERNITY IN THE PASSING MOMENT

John Schmitt

Instinct Untrammeled—
Joyous and Fearless
Nathaniel Alexander Owings

AFTER 36 YEARS OF MARRIAGE, my husband, Nat, was stricken with cancer and died in the summer of 1984, bringing to a close a pack-sack of lives, each filled with instinct and vision, creativity and leadership. All the lives he lived were filled with wonderful variables, intemperately spilling out in a great sense of humor.

I recall how he once charmed a large hall packed with people attending a symposium at the University of California. All the scholarly speakers clutched reams of papers as they spoke, reading carefully page by page.

But when Nat stepped up to the podium, he held up both hands, saying, "You'll notice I have no paper to read." (I suspect the audience was relieved.) But inadvertently brushing his upper pocket, he found a small piece of paper. Unfolding it, he announced, "I find I do have a piece of paper after all," which he proceeded to read aloud. "Bring home," I had written, "fillet of sole, and don't forget that special kind of mustard. Pick out a good cucumber and lemons and blue cheese, and of course don't neglect the sourdough bread." By the time he had finished the instructions, he had engaged the entire audience, and the lecture, I understand, went exceedingly well.

Nat was a man who believed that the hope of the future reaches back to the myths and miracles, the roots of people. When we worked together on issues of wildlife, or the guardianship of the forests, he repeatedly said, "we can do this through living in harmony with the laws of nature."

Life here in Big Sur, with the immensity of its view, taught him many things. We would stand together, looking down the coast for miles, and I could often intuitively read his mind . . . it was like the swift flight of the peregrine falcon, taking in the breadth and height of the skies and mountains, the depth and expanse of the sea, the spaces related to other spaces.

Throughout his life, Nat received many awards, from the time he graduated from his architectural training at Cornell to the founding of the partnership of Skidmore, Owings and Merrill, and later the redesigning of Pennsylvania Avenue between the White House and the Capitol in Washington, D.C. In 1983, he received the American Institute of Architects' Gold Medal, to which he responded:

"I look at the great sweep of earth and sea and mountain that is Big Sur. Is there a value placed on preserving man's sense of awe and the discovery of his right place in the universe? There is something beyond the boundaries of the limited human intellect, and that something can lead us toward truly creative energy, with new ideals and new goals to attain."

He went on to speak of the architectural firm of Skidmore, Owings and Merrill, likening it to "a peregrine falcon—feathered for space, meeting functional demands through the form of the fastest bird on earth with far-seeing eyes and sleek, windswept beauty."

Peregrines were not simply migrating birds passing through this point of land. Pairs that bred here remained here for life. But they were birds with problems they themselves could not comprehend. And had it not been for Rachel Carson's book *Silent Spring*, we might well have failed to realize what toxic sprays, including DDT or DDE, were doing to the eggshells and embryos of falcons, osprey and pelicans, not to mention human babies, children and adults. In California, in 1940, before DDT had been introduced, there were over 200 pairs of nesting peregrines, but by 1970, only two known pairs remained. Ornithologists, working from the Santa Cruz Predatory Bird Research Laboratory, set about to incubate peregrine eggs and use them to replace the broken-shelled eggs. Merlyn Felton, one of those who were deeply involved, studied these birds so meticulously that his entire life became that of the peregrine. His book *Falcons of the Rock* defined every sound, every turn of the head, their ability to catch prey in midair, and their eyesight—so powerful as to see the smallest of birds miles away. Merlyn lived with us for some time with a peregrine he called "Glass," once injured by gunshot and never to fly again.

Thus it was that our point of land, Wild Bird, became a part of the effort to reestablish the falcons along the California coast.

In May of this year, our peregrines laid three eggs. Two broke, but one hatched a healthy bird. The team from the Santa Cruz research lab went over the cliff to band the two legs of this remaining female chick with numbers large enough for the team to identify and track its movements from great distances.

A few days ago, my assistant, Joy, stepped out on the porch of her small cliff-side house and was amazed that in the bright mid-afternoon light, a small bat circled her head and then stopped, looking straight into her eyes from a few feet away. Suddenly, a falcon, swift as an arrow, seized the bat in its claws and plummeted down the precipitous cliff toward its aerie.

The image of the peregrine, in all its facets, always brings to mind my husband, even as he lay dying on his bed, with the breeze from an open window wafting across his face. It was a moment when the peregrine was very much with him, and he said: "If I have an epitaph, I want it to read 'Instinct untrammeled—joyous and fearless.'"

So much of his life was driven by instinct, and he never denied it. "Joyous" was a flower. And "fearlessly" he plunged into many dangerous endeavors.

These words describe the peregrine as if etched on the pattern of its wings. When a natural stone was carved with this powerful thought and we placed Nat's ashes beside the rock, beneath the message, a peregrine falcon cut through the air two feet above his grave, sweeping our faces with its wind.

From The Otter Raft, *No. 31, Summer 1984.*

*Rachel Carson on the dock at Woods Hole, Massachusetts, in 1951.
(Photo by Edwin Gray, Rachel Carson History Project)*

Emily Polk, (Right).
Cougar, Santa Lucia
mountains Big Sur.
(Photo by Ron Hyde)

The late Senator Fred Farr with Margaret.

Southern sea otter. (Photo by Daniel Gunther)

Margaret (left), and Lady Bird Johnson at Wild Bird, following the dedication of Bixby Creek Bridge in 1966. (Photo by Robert L. Knudsen)

Roland Clement with trumpet bird in Lima, Peru. (Photo by Carlos Saaredra Caretas)

Margaret (top), Nat Owings and Gerry Lindsay in the cliff dwellings near Bandelier, New Mexico.
(Photograph taken by Dr. George Lindsay, former director of the California Academy of Sciences.)

*Robert Redford and Margaret at Montana de Oro beach,
mid-1980s, at a resources institute meeting.*

*Nat Owings at
Keet Seel, 1983.*

Margaret at Wild Bird in Big Sur.

Dr. Jane Goodall travels all over the world to raise awareness of the plight of chimpanzees and messages of conservation. (Photo by Ken Regan)

My Days

Sweet needles, sing in the wind

Blow my hours, strain my days, rock my nights

Cling to the tossing pines

As vigorous points expand

Free, cool, clean.

My days lie like dry needles fallen

On the mountain floor

Warm brown, I tread upon them,

Shadowed black with twilight,

I lie upon them

The pages of my calendar are silver.

A WORLD VIEW

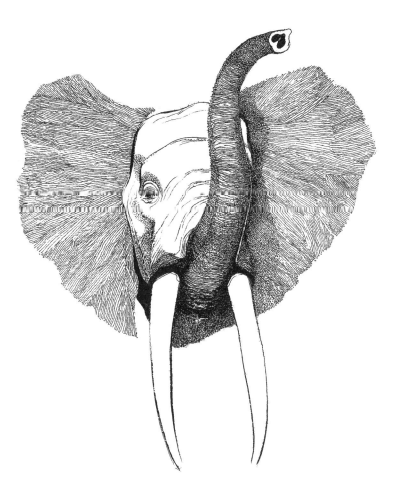

ENDANGERED SPECIES: A WORLD VIEW

Adapted from "Endangered Species: A World View," Pacific Discovery, *Vol. XXVIII, No. 1, January-February 1975, pp. 10-21. [First presented on March 1, 1974 at the annual meeting of the American Association for the Advancement of Sciences in San Francisco, California.]*

I draw your attention to a sound—

the songs of the humpback whale, the bowhead whale,
the high-pitched chirpings of the beluga whale.
Voices from threatened and disappearing life on Earth
only half-heard, only half-comprehended.
Is it a beginning, or an ending?

I draw your attention to another sound—
a repeat drumming, the roar and currents of traffic,
the shuffle and tramp of a billion feet,
a growing crescendo like massive outpourings of water: Victoria Falls,
Murchison, Niagara thundering down.
3.5 billion people today,
5.8 billion people for the year 2000.
People power!

And another sound—
the snap of a twig as wild animals disappear.
This path or that?
Selection and timing mean life or death.

The march of diminishing wildlife:
stragglers, remnants, solitaires,
and then—
nothing at all.

What forces will decide the future of wildlife?
Men with vision, foresight, intellect?
Or
Man's economy, hunger, sport, vanity, technology?
Or, to use a phrase from Loren Eiseley,
that "wounded outcry of the human ego"?

The hollow echoes sounds of the deep
flutter and groan
as heft and fluke of whales roll south.

Over the years,
is there any shifting or realigning
of these forces?
The answer is,
Yes.
But we must guard their permanence,
a permanence kept alive
only if world values change—
and hold.
That "wounded outcry of the human ego"
must reverse itself.

When one Maharaja proudly claimed
to have shot 10,000 tigers for sport—
during a period when India's tiger population
dropped from 40,000 to 2,000—
a door slammed!
And the human ego, backed into a corner,

commenced to shift its values.
The tiger, today, is India's "national animal"
with sanctuaries in 50 forests.
And the wild tiger may continue—
for a few more years.

Yes, an infinite campaign has commenced,
and one might reckon with an observation:
Suzuki Rosho, Zen Buddhist monk, remarked, before he died,
"When something is dying—it is the greatest teacher.

"During the last 150 years," says Lee Talbot,
"the rate of extermination of mammals"
(that is, the number of forms lost per unit of time)
"has increased 5.5-fold.
If this number of exterminations should continue to increase at the
same rate
it will take only 30 years
before some 4,000 out of the remaining species would be lost."

Yes—something is dying.
And—what are we learning?

First, that in this wildlife field
certain wildlife habitats must have areas of complete isolation
without intrusion from Man.
But where, we might ask,
does the delicate demarcation line lie,
between intrusion and isolation?

For example,
should we advocate that selected portions
of the Galápagos Islands

be left undisturbed by increasing numbers of tourist trips? Is this a needed safeguard
against interruptions into the natural rhythms of the rookeries,
and unintentional trodding on the eggs of the iguana?

Or, wasn't Scammon's Lagoon an example
of what was a growing nightmare intrusion
into the major breeding and calving waters of the gray whale? In 1971
the Mexican government declared the lagoon a sanctuary—
followed by further protective regulations.
Commercial whale-watching boats,
as well as private yachts previously granted access,
are no longer permitted into the lagoon,
and the road now carries certain disciplined uses
along the shallow waters of the shore.

But Karl Kenyon's Christmas letter
recounts an aerial survey for the Caribbean monk seal
over the Gulf of Mexico and the Caribbean Sea.
It revealed that this seal is now extinct.
Extinct—we ask why.
"Because," said Kenyon,
"Man has now invaded the most remote atolls and islets
that were the final refuge where remnant populations existed."

Yes, there is a dire need for further isolation,
where far-flung waves on lonely shores shift sand.
A need for breeding areas,
a need for incubation nurseries
as undisturbed as the embryo.

Another episode that lies across our path
is brushed by a dark wing.
The California condor,

reduced to a number between 30 and 40 birds,
is vulnerable to any disturbance in its nesting area.
With the establishment of the Sespe Condor Refuge
in the Los Padres National Forest, in 1947,
it was hoped that the 60 birds counted at that time
would increase.
Instead, their numbers declined.
Strychnine bait for coyotes and ignorant trigger-happy hunters
were thought to be the causes of death.

But other reasons hampered their survival.
Although this particular region—
where upcurrents of air can lift a 20-pound body
and a nine-foot spread of wings—
was closed and guarded by a warden,
it still remained impossible to keep prospectors out. Pressures for
recreational use
and oil-drilling considerations
continue to intrude into the nesting area.
In addition, scientists, checking nests,
may have caused further interference.
Nests used in the past are now abandoned.
Today, it is thought,
there may be only one or two active condor nests.
The complete isolation needed for survival
appears impossible for man to comprehend.

Under the federal government
refuges and sanctuaries are established as "long term solutions."
But what is a "long term"?
Is it the life of a politician in office?

When experiments in technology or resource exploitation
move into these sacrosanct regions

not only with government permission
but with economic aid for encouragement,
power-pressures are clearly at the top of the value scale. Perhaps this
is a resemblance to the bull elephant seal leaving the beach when the
alarm bell rings,
trampling and extinguishing the lives of young pups.
Both are forms of diminished vision—
and mass stampede.

Amchitka Island and the Arctic National Wildlife Refuge
are examples of disquieting warnings.
Amchitka—a national wildlife refuge since 1913
and a sea otter refuge since 1936—
but, you know the story:
28 years later the Atomic Energy Commission took the island for a
test site;
five years later, another explosion;
followed by the 1971 Cannikin blast
that killed an estimated 1,000 to 1,330 sea otters.
We called this a "Sanctuary."

The 8.9 million acres of the Arctic National Wildlife Refuge
were an outpost,
we thought,
for wolves, grizzly bears, polar bears, moose and caribou, with only
natives permitted to use the wildlife resources.
But the door was left ajar
and the white man crisscrossed the slopes with bulldozer and truck,
poached wolves for recreation.
And today, with further encroachment,
the exploratory drilling for gas
is permitted to ravish the land with big equipment.

"When something is dying . . . " what has this teacher taught us?

A second point:
that a cautiously planned and balanced percentage of the Earth's
surface—
land and water—
will have to remain inviolate,
untouched by technology,
if we are to preserve any form of free-moving wildlife on this globe.
Without this foresight
the great freedoms will be gone;
territories, lost,
migrations, halted;
and acknowledged tensions that keep a wild community stable will be
fractured.

The terms "threatened" or "endangered"
are directly associated with two more troubling words today:
"acceleration" and "excess"—
an ugly team marching into
what we might have called
the Age of Ecology.

Due to this acceleration, and excess of greed,
mammals in some regions
could be approaching a "near extinction" category
before the issue is fully grasped
by Man.

An example is the elephant and its ivory.
In Kenya, during 1974, it has been estimated
that more than 1,000 elephants are poached each month.
Even a small elephant's tusks can bring $2,000.
Ivory is gold; gold is walking around in the bush;
the world market is wide open.
And the native Africans silently emerge from the bush

bearing ivory across their shoulders at $45.00 a pound.
Dead bodies lie neglected.
Patrols are inadequate.
Although Kenya is now counting its remaining elephants
while all elephant hunting is banned,
and Tanzania has placed a ban on all game,
and Zaire stopped elephant hunting last year,
and the Ivory Coast established a moratorium
on hunting elephants,
these measures stop legal hunting
but excessive poaching appears to be accelerating—
and the world market receives it.

Yes, again, something is dying—
defining for us a third regulation for preservation of wildlife,
that the strong arm of an international warden
be implemented through an effective system
of international world order,
financed, trained, and equipped for service around the world to police
conservation measures
necessary for endangered wildlife survival
and its threatened habitat.
For the view is a world view now,
and the destruction of wildlife
can no longer be considered a local right
for people wishing to protect local
and personal interests.

Perhaps the taking of a million sea otters for their furs
during a century and a half of slaughter
resulted in the illusion of a stable superabundance of shellfish
along the California coastal shelf.
For the otters had occupied these waters for thousands of years,
and an ecological balance existed among

the abalone, sea urchin, crab and otter—
a balance markedly disturbed by the otters' near extinction.
For, as Estes and Palmisano found
through studies on the otters' role in structuring nearshore communities,
this sea mammal is an evolutionary component
essential to the integrity and stability of the ecosystem.

During the otters' death blow
any cumulative backlog of shellfish was quickly reaped
by commercial exploitation of abalone,
which outstripped the resource and then moved on.

Yet as the otters gradually returned
it was they who were blamed
for the drastic reduction of the shellfish.
With the California Department of Fish and Game
keyed to commercial and sport use of a resource,
the issue of the otters was defined
not as a rarity, back from near extinction
but as a predator in competition with Man.
Today, with calculated risks of oil spills
from increasing tanker traffic and growing toxic wastes draining into the sea,
the otters could face an abrupt threat to their existence.

It is for this reason that we look
to the nation's Marine Mammal Commission,
with its scientific advisory board,
for the judgment on a wildlife issue
that could not otherwise have become disentangled
from the local market catch of shellfish
or the 430 percent increase in skin diving in the last decade.
We look for a broader valuation

than the state is capable of focusing on.
We look for an outlook into the future.
We look for a world view.

But to complete this circle of thought
I return to the whales,
to the rising of signs.
The fact that Japan claims their whaling operations are conducted
"not only to maintain" but "to increase" the whale population,
clearly presents the need
for unbiased facts and world enforcement.
As Scott McVeigh speaks out:
"The largest brains on Earth,
gloriously unique in the scheme of things—
these whales will be gone
before man may be able to understand them."

THE HUMPBACK WHALE SINGS

The hollow echoed soundings of the deep,
Flutter and groan,
As heft and fluke of whales roll south.

These gray-lit waters stir and lift and fall,
The low, slow voices rumble and explode,
The lonely velvet note so grave, so tall,
Will bend itself along the darkened road.

Exhaled the song is sung—the circle closed,
The scale then mounts on rhythmic silver wings
And once again, the pod in chorus, blows
And in a moment's grace—creation sings.

The whales belay the flute with muted strings
And tip their creaking vessels as they pass.

PASSING THE TORCH

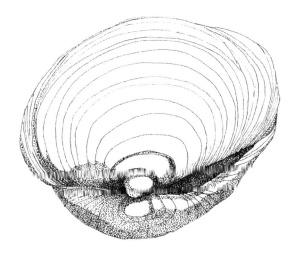

In Defense of Natural Systems

Adapted from a presentation to the 37th North American Wildlife and Natural Resources Conference Technical Session, "Preservation: Peril or Panacea?" Mexico City, Mexico, 1970.

I SPEAK AS A LAYMAN, one person out of the vast growing assemblage of conservation-minded citizens. I am one of those citizens who place high value on wildlife in its natural state in a propitious environment and do not care to kill it.

I am oriented toward the preservation of wildlife rather than toward its exploitation for commercial gain, sport-killing for recreation and the ingrained theory that wildlife is useless unless it is used. I am concerned about the gratification of our greed.

I carry a distrust of management programs, which frequently impress me as systems to subjugate and subdue. Some might consider them practical solutions, mathematical equations that balance life against life, a controlled world without blemish. I favor the necessary studies to carry out research on shifting situations in wildlife populations and habitat, if the study itself does not damage the studied. I am aware that the biological imbalance already brought about by man can sometimes be rectified by some management—including the management of man himself. Invariably, out of wildlife studies come management proposals for manipulation from the complex to the simple. Is this a step forward or backward?

My introduction to wildlife management took place along the border of the Los Padres National Forest, California, in high ridge country laced only by a fire road. It was the early 1950s when I was hiking along an animal trail with my dog. A government vehicle appeared and braked to a stop to warn me that I had better pick up my dog, since traps and cyanide guns had just been set out. Quite naturally, I asked the man what they were after. The answer was "predators," because they had just introduced a dozen wild turkeys into the area and wanted to clear the region of the birds' natural enemies.

I didn't need an education in science to recognize that protection of exotic game targets for sportsmen through extermination of predators upon which the natural system depended was wrong. From that moment on, I took a new look. I paid attention to government agencies and their bureaus and the pressures that directed their activities.

Administrators of natural resources, I found, usually claim that their decisions are in the public interest. This public interest, however, is subject to opinions based on self-interest and reflects dominant groups. A major criterion for determining public interest is often not related to quality perspective or long-view consequences but, instead, is based on numbers of people, sums of money and associated commercial enterprises.

Who are the dominant groups that direct the administration of wildlife in California? Since few in the Department of Fish and Game are charged with maintaining wildlife for the enjoyment of citizens who do not care to kill, the dominant groups to receive attention are the Associated Sportsmen and the California Wildlife Federation—the hunting public. Though the public owns the game, the Department of Fish and Game, supported mainly by funds which accrue from hunting and fishing licenses, duck stamps, wetland stamps and the Pittman-Robertson tax, serves primarily to enhance this game for the 763,284 hunters and 2,323,847 fishermen whose fees pay the bills.

Thus, approximately 3 million out of some 20 million citizens in the state direct the wildlife program, sending their lobbies into the legislative sessions and penetrating in depth the administration of the department. But a counterbalance to this California self-serving pressure group has sprung out of a growing revolution of public attitude and a sudden astonished awareness that the law reads: "Wildlife is the property of the people, the sovereignty of which they have vested in the state to conserve and manage for the benefit of all the people."

What has brought about this change in public attitude? The recognition of a deteriorating environment and the growing comprehension of the word "ecology"? Or the impact of the long view—our planet in space, in MacLeish's words, "small and blue and beautiful in the eternal silence in which it floats?" Or is there a growing intimate sense of loss as the news media and television present endangered species with quality photography illustrating animals in action in the systems in which they live?

Whatever the stimulus, a fresh concept is taking hold that wildlife is there, that it is part of us, that we are part of it, that all life is an extension of ourselves. And out of it, a new form of recreation is evolving that takes nothing away—observing wildlife with binoculars and recording it with lens, describing it in writing and participating as individuals in the act of appreciation and the effort of preservation.

In California, these people have grown increasingly uneasy and impatient with the administration of the Department of Fish and Game and with its handling of certain of the state's distinguished mammals. These people are organizing and have taken their concerns to their legislators, and they have found a responsive body at the capitol to introduce restrictive legislation for the protection of wildlife. In addition, these people have defeated special-interest bills favorable to Fish and Game programs.

In the spring of 1970, the foremost issue pertaining to a special-interest group became, in simple terms, a matter of values.

Where do you place your value, the public was asked—on a small gourmet industry, the red abalone? Or do you place it on a rare marine mammal, the southern sea otter?

California Senate Bill 442, pressured by the abalone industry and approved by the Department of Fish and Game, was introduced to solve the sea otter and commercial abalone controversy. Although the population count of the fully protected southern sea otter, *Enhydra lutris nereis*, was 1,014, this bill allowed sea otters to be "taken outside the California Sea Otter Refuge," providing there was a public hearing before the Fish and Game Commission.

The public was quick to discover that the word "take" could mean "kill" and that one-third of the total southern sea otter population lived outside the refuge. Although the 100-mile refuge, established by legislative act soon after the otters were rediscovered in 1938, was to protect otters, not to limit their movements, the reading of the bill suggested otherwise.

Placed in the category of competitors for the red abalone, the otter was blamed for the decline of an industry which was suffering, in great part, from its own overharvesting. In addition, the abalone resource was declining along the entire California coast, much of which was far from the otter's range. Although the otter is skilled in extracting abalones from underwater rocks, he does so with time, effort and many dives. He also eats some 26 other items of food which he procures more easily.

As the facts unfolded, the bill became an educational process for the public. Their admiration for the otter's charms grew, as did their understanding of his complex role in marine ecology. Since otters are the chief harvesters of the sea urchin, the absence of otters in southern California waters had permitted the urchins to multiply unhindered. Since the sea urchins destroy kelp, they affect the vast community of marine life dependent upon it, including the abalone. Thus, the public learned about the subtle life-relationships that link marine organisms to one another and to their surroundings.

Amended at the last minute to remove the world "take" and substitute "catch, capture, or pursue," the bill moved into the public hearings phase, where it was backed by the sportsmen's lobby and the California Wildlife Federation. "Speaking for more than 800,000 people, whom we represent in California," they said, "this is a very good piece of legislation."

But the informed and serious conservation groups placed their values with the otters, bombarded their legislators, and defeated the bill. Dr. Robert T. Orr, associate director of the California Academy of Sciences, summed up the issue when he testified at the hearing.

"We are living in an age when our nation is becoming very conservation-minded, trying to undo the great damage that man has done to his environment. Senate Bill 442 is so far out of tune with this concept that it might well have been conceived in the 19th century. It proposes to curb sea otters, which are barely past the danger point. And why? So that a small group of market hunters, commercializing something that belongs to all of us, can continue their exploitation to produce a gourmet item."

After the defeat of this ill-advised bill, it appeared to many of us that Fish and Game continued a devaluation of the southern sea otter when it refused to recommend placing this animal on the state's "Rare and Endangered List." With its population dangerously low, this subspecies of the more populous northern sea otter, *Enhydra lutris*, is vulnerable to residues of mercury, cadmium, copper and zinc in the marine life on which it feeds as well as pollution from pesticides, toxic wastes and raw sewage. Continual harassment by commercial abalone divers (approximately 50 deaths in two years), as well as propeller lacerations from increasing boat activities (27 deaths attributed), added to the unceasing threat of oil spills from tanker traffic, would indicate small assurance of safety for this unique marine mammal.

Was Fish and Game's negative recommendation influenced not by these facts but by the fact that their own hands could be tied in carrying out a management program if the otters were placed on the Rare and Endangered List?

Government stewardship to guard a diversity of wildlife for the benefit of all the people has floundered too often and too long. Without a game label, wildlife is tossed into the "varmint" category—an easy target for the man with the gun. Fish and Game admits that it knows nothing of nongame distribution. "Little has been done for nongame either in research or management."[1]

Yet these animals, such as the bobcat and coyote, increase the efficiency of life as a part of the ecosystem. Whether it be prey or predator, man moves in with carnage. A recent aerial broadcasting of grain soaked in 1080 poison in Fresno and San Luis Obispo counties in California brought this justification from the agricultural commissioner: "It is no longer feasible," he wrote, "to control ground squirrels with coyotes and rattlesnakes."[2]

I have made reference to hunting, which is approved by law as a recognized form of recreation. Men purchase arms from the munitions industry and equipment from the sporting goods market, buy licenses and stamps from the government and go out in trucks at prescribed dates according to regulations and shoot game they do not need for food. There are exceptions, of course, when game may serve as an indispensable food requirement, but these are rare. Hunting augments the economy, which is a factor in its political power, and according to Ed Zern, outdoor writer for *Field and Stream*, it answers a "psychic need."[3]

What is this psychic need? Is it to proclaim man's dominion over life? To fell a great tree? To dam a wild river? To cut down a strong free animal in action? I call it an uneven contest, this use of steel and fire, and neither tradition nor its legality make it benign.

Mr. Zern claims that nonhunters refuse to accept death as an essential part of life. Yet how can man refuse or accept death unless he himself is prey? What predator stalks the hunter's trail in North America?

But I am not here to moralize about hunting. Many sportsmen carry their own code of ethics and carefully follow the law as it is defined. There are others, however, with gun racks in their pickups who need only a moving target. Within sight of our house in Big Sur, these hunters have gunned down great blue herons on the shore; does giving birth, and even Steller sea lions. We watched it happen. The trucks move on. They are what Ian McHarg would call "vandals of our storehouse."

Although Howard Leach, California wildlife management supervisor, said, "We realize how unknowledgeable we are concerning the status of California's nongame animals, particularly those in short supply." The California mountain lion, moved from the nongame category into big game status, caused Fish and Game, without preliminary studies, to begin selling an unrestricted number of one-dollar permits to hunt lions in any season, day or night, either sex, young or old; to use dogs. and no game limit on the hunter.

At this time, when the world is closing in on wildlife from all sides, Fish and Game, without any study to substantiate it, made a flat statement: "The lion's population," they said, "is stable." "To base management policy on guesswork," wrote George Schaller to the Natural Resource Committee on May 21, 1971, "is a sad state of affairs in a state with as large a game department staff as California.

With the cougar's wild habitat increasingly accessible to skilled hunters and trained dogs, discrete lion populations could be eliminated. Before the year was over, the state had sold 4,746 lion permits to prospective hunters. "As long as we keep on killing them, there must be lions left"[4] was the only possible theory under which this game program could operate.

In the early months of the 1971 program, Assembly Bill 660 was introduced to stop the sport-killing of lions and provide for the take and capture of lions causing depredation. The public, perceiving an acceleration of the decline of this beautiful animal, was challenged into vigorous action.

How can a lion population be stable, they asked, when hunting itself is not stable? The California Fish and Wildlife Plan in 1964 stated that "there are probably no more than 100 individuals who make an effort to hunt lions," yet, suddenly in 1971, 4,746 hunters were to enter the field seeking a big game trophy.

Over 50 conservation organizations banded together with a preservation platform that covered the state with its message. In alarm, the chairman of the state Fish and Game Commission called it "tunnel vision." As the conservationists carried the bill through the assembly, the California Wildlife Federation wrote their members, "Once again, the antihunting people are threatening our sport."

In the meantime, the Fish and Game Commission, on guard, passed new, cautious regulations for the coming season on lions, permitting only 50 lions to be shot during a limited season, with certain areas closed to hunting. But the conservation-minded citizens had been challenged. They were not assured—and in a massive manner, they pressed the amended bill through the legislature. Defying the California Wildlife Federation, the bill reached the governor's desk, procured his signature and made it into law.

As Dr. A. Starker Leopold remarked, "If the department cannot accept the change of public attitude toward wildlife and respond to these pressures, everything will consequently go the legislative route." Mr. Leach echoed this opinion when he concluded a department paper with this warning: "We better get wired into the environment issue of the day, or someone else will take our place."

Yes, someone else will take your place and will bring a halt the lopsided program dealing primarily with game animals that fails outright to strengthen or protect wildlife as a whole.

With the biota losing its structure and wildlife populations shrinking, the federal and state agencies must be reminded for the final time that the public, not the sportsmen, own the game and nongame animals.

This public voice, as yet an unharnessed strength, will prevail—and newly established wildlife agencies, oriented in training for a guardianship role, will replace the present bureaus, financed by funds from general taxation as well as a share of the sportsmen's fees and a preservation license purchased by citizens across the nation.

Out of the 37th North American Conference, this single imperative change must evolve. It calls for a decisive move into new directions of wildlife husbandry by both state and federal agencies.

[1] Dr. Aryan Roest, "Systematic study of the sea otter, *Enhydra lutris*. October 23, 1971. Blosonor Conference, Menlo Park, California

2 Howard Leach, "California's Endangered Wildlife: 1971 Joint Conference," California-Nevada Section Wildlife Society.

3 Zern, Ed. "I Am a Hunter." *Audubon* Magazine, January, 1972.

[4] Gilbert, Bill. "A Close Look at Wildlife." *American Environment Life* Magazine Series

HAMMOCKS

"To find eternity in the passing moment."

—Lancelot Whyte

IN MY MIND'S EYE, I've been carrying for 20 years a broad cord-woven hammock stretched out 50 feet below our house on the cliff. It is strung 550 feet above the sea and can swing slowly and gently over sage and lichened rocks and a bit of cypress before the perpendicular drop to the sea below. The updraft scent of kelp and brine plays a chord with the sounds of waters broken by honking sea lions and, seasonally, the sharp knife-cut in the air as peregrine falcons speed over my hammock and dive down to their aerie, where young chicks wait to be fed.

Those words by Romain Gary, "The sea, the original breeder of us all" repeat themselves in the rhythm of my hammock as a broad V of brown pelicans flies north in steady outline, disappearing beyond our point. Oh, the bird's-eye view of the immensity of the woven pattern of migrating whales, of coastal sea mammals, fish and pelagic birds with tides in their veins!

Through my binoculars, I have watched, by the hour, sea otters emerging from a dive on the edge of our rich kelp bed, a continent of life. They roll and twist in the fronds to stabilize themselves as their front paws grasp a clam or an abalone to crack on rock tools placed on their chests. On silent evenings, despite the distance, I have heard the tap-tap breaking of the shell as well as the high-pitched cry of a waiting pup. Even silence spills its secrets.

But a modified hammock was mine to encounter this past October when Dr. James Mattison, Jr., with whom I founded Friends of the Sea Otter, brought his wife, Joanne, and several kayaks to the

Monterey Coast Guard ramp. It was in recognition of my resignation as president of our organization after 22 years. There we met two of our new trustees and slipped the narrow, pointed kayaks out onto the quiet waters of Monterey Bay. Mist was rising as we glided toward a raft of three otters, holding their hind flippers out of the water like open fans. Two white faces were rubbing together, while the third rose high from the surface and gave us its full attention. Eye-level, we shared an intimate vision.

Rounding the stony breakwater, we slid past extravagant, quarreling sea lions and a strong smell of fish. On water that was like glass, we glided over shoreline shallows of sand and stone. An orange sea star closed in on its prey as close-knit anemones spread their tentacles from the rocks. I rested my paddle and passed my hand through the water to pick up strands of kelp, one bearing turban snails, another a limpet—sea otter hors d'oeuvres. Abruptly we were surrounded by harbor seals that came directly beside us, their big eyes holding our own in a magnetic exchange, strong whiskers and spotted fur. Tactile adventures at eye level.

When we pulled our kayaks up onto a small rocky beach for our "kayak picnic," migrating monarch butterflies floated around us, drawn perhaps by our colors, one landing on a shoulder.

We talked about the otters. Together we had counted 12. We turned our attention to a female nearby, low in the water, sculling along with an enormous pup draped heavily across her belly. The mother was close to drowning. I studied her with binoculars. "That's me!" I cried—followed by laughter. For I had long sought a replacement for my role—and herewith, I saw it clearly. The simplest things in nature are full of meaning. I have now passed the mantle of responsibility on to a fine group of trustees, a single functionary unit, though I will always carry a close moral and spiritual contact with Friends of the Sea Otter.

From The Otter Raft, *No. 44, Winter 1990-91.*

ARTS AND NATURE

GEORGIA O'KEEFFE

IT WAS IN 1976 that Ansel and Virginia Adams brought Georgia
O'Keeffe down to our house in Big Sur. It was a beautiful afternoon,
and one could sense the immensity of the coast and catch the glitter
of the water and view the silhouettes of the Santa Lucia mountains
plunging down into the surf.

Georgia O'Keeffe was wearing her signature black-brimmed hat.
She asked me if she could be given a tablet to sketch what lay before
her. I ran down to my small studio, built below the edge of the cliff,
and came up with a fresh drawing tablet and some dark pencils. I
watched her as she began to draw. It wasn't a sketch, it was strong,
solid lines which included some of the A-frame of our redwood
house. Nat was delighted to have her here, and it was all a happy
medley, until Georgia stood up and asked where I'd brought this
tablet from. I told her I had a studio, and she announced that she
wanted to go down there.

Now, it may not seem important to many people, but it suddenly
seemed important to me that Georgia O'Keeffe not see my studio
filled with spiderwebs, heaps of artwork and stained windows. So I
told her the path was too dangerous. This, naturally, was an insult.
She turned to me and said, "I can climb up and down ladders, which I
do every day."

So I began a new tactic and said, "It's filled with spiderwebs and
everything is out of order; I just open the door and push things in."
She answered, "So do I," then added, "If you let me see your studio,
I'll let you see my storage room for paintings. I cross the courtyard

and unlock the door and open it about four inches and push in my paintings. Then I quickly lock the door and go back to the house." She was already halfway down the crooked stone steps at this point, and I realized I had lost. As we reached the door, she added, "Call me the next time you go out to your place in New Mexico and I'll invite you out to see my storage room."

And what did she find in my studio, you might ask? Exactly what I had warned her about. But her eyes immediately fell on a number of bird skulls we had found on an island in the Sea of Cortez. She ignored a few paintings hanging on the wall but liked my black-and-white brush-and-ink paintings of cormorants and stones and shells along with Sierra granite.

A few months later, when we were out in New Mexico, she invited me to lunch.

Her assistant Juan was there and remarked, "Aren't you going to ask Georgia if she's going to show you her storage room?" I replied that it was on my mind but I hardly dared ask, and I wasn't sure she had remembered.

"Does she remember!" he exclaimed. "Let's cross the courtyard and see."

Yes, here it was, locked, with a burglar alarm attached. Juan undid these, then opened the door and turned on the light. Everything was painted white, and there was a huge table covered with white oilcloth on which she could place her paintings to wrap or unwrap them. Everything was perfect!

"But this isn't fair! I showed you my studio only because you told me about your messy studio." Juan looked down at her, then looked over at me. "She's been working on this room all morning in preparation for your coming." We had a good laugh over that.

O'Keeffe was losing her sight, and over the years we were to see her often, but we never mentioned it, nor did she. Over the fireplace in her large workroom hung a very black painting which she told me followed an operation on her eyes. While she was lying unconscious on the table, all of a sudden she saw a light in the center of the blackness, and it brought back her life again. She loved this painting and so did I.

Out in New Mexico, the colors and shadows change every hour of the day. She recognized this, and like a big clock, the shadows told her when to climb her ladder to the roof, or walk out with her cane and two dogs through the scrub pine toward the barancas.

One afternoon when she was with us, we walked over to the terrace where she had first spotted my studio. Suddenly, she turned to Nat and said, "I want this house. I want you to will me this house." Then she glanced over at me to see what my reaction was and laughed with a kind of sly look in her eyes. It was a delightful, laughing look, rarely seen on the face of this enigmatic, talented woman. "Better watch out," Juan warned me. "Georgia gets everything she has ever asked for." From then on, we joked quite a bit about it and often referred to it as "Georgia's house."

Georgia almost always wore her black felt hat and would hardly go anyplace without it. One afternoon, when we were all together, Juan joked that Georgia was going to give him the hat someday. "With that, he lifted it off her head and placed it on his own. It wasn't at all right for Juan, so he put it on Nat's head. But Nat had an enormous head, and it made the hat look very tiny. I removed it from Nat's head and put it on mine. Need I tell you, it was a perfect fit? So I told Georgia that since she was getting Nat's house in his will, she should will me her hat!

One of Georgia's last notes to us spoke warmly of her times in our lovely Big Sur. "Juan and I were speaking of you the day your letter arrived," she wrote. "We had thought of how fine it would be to visit your home in the clouds above the ocean."

COMPLETING THE CIRCLE AT MILLS COLLEGE

"..whose artist's eye sees to the heart of living things, and whose untiring guardianship of forgotten citizens of California—the sea otter and sea lion, the mountain lion and redwood—has been steadfast and ever green as the Monterey Pines on the coast she loves.."

—Trustees of Mills College

Adapted from an acceptance speech upon receiving an honorary doctorate degree at Mills College, May 23, 1993.

INTERESTINGLY ENOUGH, THIS AWARD completes a circle in my house of life. And today, I look up at that dormer window on the third floor of Mills Hall, where every 15 minutes the chimes once pealed loudly and rolled through my open window.

Was it the announcement of a new world? For Mills, at that time, was almost an island, a foothold from which new life developed. New attitudes, new interests, new causes, new learning, new friends— and a new sense of values. But "no man is an island," John Donne wrote. Nor, for that matter, is any living thing an island. For me, Mills is a strong, water-worn stone on which one stands before diving into swift and dangerous waters.

The dangerous waters roar with the sounds of traffic and the shuffle of a million feet: technology; nuclear power; international television and war, as well as human generosity and caring. But it was here at Mills that I found art, an oasis, an unexplored landscape. And art can be magic—a reckless moment of freedom to be cultivated. Art, music and literature—the great joys of life. And add to them wilderness and wildlife, each carries a renewing sense, and meanings that were elusive suddenly become clear. Each should be treasured in the same way. Yes, art and nature go hand in hand. With a gratitude for the privilege of living on our land, this century, this decade, this year, this moment of time. And with a conscience for life consider—

How many warnings do we need?

How many proofs?

How many deaths?

How much beauty gone?—

before we send out a lifeline, not alone for wildlife and wilderness, but for quality and aesthetic considerations and for ethical purposes (since man is the predator).

Yes, art and nature walk hand in hand. And as the campanile bell chimes each hour, time escalates into the future for Mills College, and I, for one, returning here following my 80th birthday, complete a circle today.

Thank you.

Pumas, Wolves, Films and Robert Redford

It was in August, 1985, that I received a phone call from a man with a special voice who said right away, "I'm so glad to reach you. I've been wanting to talk to you for two years." I had no idea who he was, so I waited. "This is Robert Redford," he said.

He went on to say that he had been putting out environmental brushfires since 1971, and he wanted to see some culmination to it. Although I had never met him, I had read from time to time that he was trying to keep uranium from being mined on the border of Zion National Park, and that he was also trying to block the construction of an enormous road near where he was building his place at Sundance. But the people in Utah turned against him, sending threatening notes to his wife and children and burning him in effigy. So he closed the door on that particular chapter and started what he called a resource management institute, including representatives from both sides of an issue. He invited me to attend the next meeting, and I agreed.

Previously, I had heard him speak on television, talking about the condor. I had thought, at the time, he had handled it just perfectly, and so I took this opportunity to tell him so. And I remembered when, in 1970, a government-mandated program in Alaska involved shooting wolf packs from planes or catching them by traps, it was Robert Redford who narrated a public service announcement on PBS accompanied by a film of wolves.

Redford's commanding voice spoke these words:

> We know he lives because we hear the howl.
> But today, that howl is heard less and less.
> Soon, he will have no territories to return to.
> Soon, his kind will disappear.
> And the splendid creature,
> this living machine that has triumphed
> for ten thousand millennia,
> will follow other species into the absolute,
> irreversible, emptiness of extinction.

In October, 1985, I directed Robert's attention to one of my chief concerns:

"As you must have heard, Governor Deukmejian vetoed the mountain lion bill, and although it was already dismembered and drained of every protective measure for the lion because of the governor's amendments (directed by the NRA), we still were anxious to have it pass because it would leave us a small toehold. Mountain lions will be on the trophy list by the first of the year."

Meanwhile, the California Department of Fish and Game was carrying out an "experimental research study" to exterminate every lion within a 250-mile range of the North Fork of the Kings River over a four-year period. The reason, mind you, was to see if the lion was the cause of the deer decline.

"But why am I writing you, Robert? Because I sense you would have a strong response to this form of wildlife destruction. We want to reach the public with full impact, and I must confess, I flashed on a vision of your face on a 60-second vignette for television, with a few chosen words from you to accompany a wild lion climbing a tree. We have the films and are lining up space on television, but we need you! It's not a 'brushfire'—but the survival of our greatest symbol of wilderness in California."

Robert wrote back, "I have finished the filming of *The Milagro Beanfield War* and am editing the film here at Sundance. It was a beautiful agony, making the film. I'm both glad and sorry it is over. I look forward to telling you about it. I hope to see you soon. I will plan to drop by sometime within the month and see if birds still sing at your porch."

Redford had come to our house several times during the filming, telling me about how he had made a star of our 1952 Chevy truck from our ranch in New Mexico. It had a bullet hole through the windshield, and the window-wipers rarely worked. Its only modification for the film was the purchase of new tires so that the film audience could hear crunching over gravel. "It's as important to the movie as any of the actors," announced Redford. I felt flattered. Robert could always make a high art of a compliment. One day, he brought actress Sonia Braga to the house. They arrived with baskets of food and then ran down the surfers path to the beach. When they returned, I was given seven white stones to be arranged on our dining table, four from Robert and three from Sonia. Robert arranged them himself with a sprig of paintbrush.

I had sent Redford a poem I had written many years ago about the town of Truchas in the Sangre de Cristo range. It was the town that was the setting for *The Milagro Beanfield War*. He told me he had thumbtacked it up on the wall by his desk.

Truchas

No keys to close these doors of isolation,
Pathless gates and shafts of broken dwellings,
Where dregs of wine stain floorboards
And pale blue walls stand to crumble
The frenzied echo of night riders
Crushing splinters of silent crosses
As the church stands idle.

Where have they gone
Splintered sorrows, sky-written dreams
Now deep in tangled grasses
And a foot below?
Pressed by hoofs in the foolish laughter
But the hungers still rise windblown.

Oh meet me there
By the dark cornice,
By the spider's shadow,
By the flutter of torn muslin.
Old desires lie broken—and I'm alone
Tormenting unsought—for memories.

In March, 1991, Robert told me about another project he was working on, which he referred to as "a small film in Montana. He sent me the book, *A River Runs Through It*. "Read it," he told me. "You will hear a special voice. I hope to bring it to the screen. He continued, "Tonight's full moon makes me think of what it must be like on your porch. How I envy, at least, the thought of it. Following 'like a big yellow dog,'" as e.e. cummings says, replete with occasional breath from offshore flows and the constant barking from the rocks below."

I enjoyed the story a great deal and felt its last line rang so true: "Eventually, all things merge into one, and a river runs through it." I wrote my enthusiastic approval to Robert.

He wrote back, "What a wonderful gift your letter was, so full of good news. Of course I am pleased that you liked the film. In the end, provoking such a response is, I think, the final reward. And how lovely the ink painting is. I will cherish its presence, as it carries as much that is unique. In the meantime, dear Margaret, your notes are tonic. I am always lifted by either a word or a visit. I look forward to a visit soon. The coast must be beautiful about now. Cool and clear and less populated by the infernal visits of the curious. A time for weather and animals, when nature expresses its powerful love. A love so often missed by so many who need it."

Years later, in April, 1996, I visited Sundance, an inspiration, with water running over the stones with such vitality, and snow reaching down the peaks to touch our front doorstep.

The conference at Sundance was to bridge the gap between children's health and the environment. Nancy and Jim Chuda had lost their five-year-old daughter, Colette, to cancer and their sorrow was so great that they found life very difficult until they saw more clearly that a purpose lay before them. They dedicated their lives to guarding other children from toxins in the environment, these unrecognized carcinogens which had also reached their close friend, Olivia Newton-John, who struggled through breast cancer. It changed her life to a deeper understanding. She produced a new record called *Gaia*, filled with strong words for our earth and how it must be kept pure for the sake of our loved ones.

I received an environmental achievement award, and in my acceptance speech I said, "Man is cutting the threads of the fabric with no thought of the consequences." I emphasized the work of Rachel Carson, who died of cancer while trying to stop the world from using toxic sprays on agriculture-toxins that entered our food chain and contaminated the water and the air we breathe. Yes, it is a "silent spring" when the birds cease to sing.

Robert wrote a letter which Olivia read aloud before I read my statement. He was unable to attend, because he was filming the massive snowstorm that caused the tragic accident at the beginning of his film *The Horse Whisperer*—a noble film!

An assortment of individuals attended the conference, many of whom came from remote parts of the country. I found myself seated beside a man named Joe Henry, whose talents emerged as we talked. He saw through the visible surface of things and I soon realized that he was a songwriter and a poet. I learned that he had received many awards for special events like the Olympic games opening words, but he was indifferent to them. I asked him for his card. He pulled an old wallet from his pocket saying, "I have no card," but took out a photograph of an old horse and said, "This is my family."

Holding the folder for the symposium in my hand, I studied it for the first time, and viewed a photograph of a little girl about five years old, not unlike Colette, climbing up a rugged stone face. A poem by Joe Henry accompanied it, and the last line echoed the proud cause of the conference, "like the flower that shattered the stone."

THE SHINING HOUR

THERE ARE THOSE WHO REGARD the sea primarily as a dimension, an immensity, a grand proportion with the horizon, stretching to eternity. These people think by expansion—the broad, deep picture they find rewarding. And among the largest of sea mammals on this planet, 20,000 gray whales, once driven nearly to extinction by the hands of man, now migrate each year from Alaska south to Baja, returning with their newborn young, skirting the California coast, blowing their fountains as they pass—appropriate symbols of the larger view.

There are those who turn to the intimate savor of the sea, where an otter somersaults, then turns gracefully down between the kelp strands in a melodic manner. These people find their reward in the detailed focus on this smallest sea mammal, a life with undeniable strength but vulnerable to stress, pollution and man. Let us then reflect for a moment upon the dynamic ability of these creatures to bring into focus an ethical philosophy which truly can act as a powerful restraint upon man's violations of the marine ecology.

How often do we find selflessness and human generosity when it relates to sea mammals such as these? Can livelihood be tempered when it turns to these rare beings? Can a conscience in life be instilled quite suddenly to rise to an emergency measure, as it did when Roy Ahmaogak, an Eskimo whaler from Point Barrow, Alaska, found three gray whales trapped in a small pool that was rapidly freezing over in subzero weather? The desperate whales were raising their heads, breathing out to cry for help. One was to slip under the ice and die as rescue work commenced. The Eskimo whalers used chain saws to cut breathing holes, creating an irresistible momentum that quickly touched the conscience of the world. Then came helicopters with five-ton wrecking balls to crack the ice, followed by a Soviet icebreaker, which painfully cut a passage through ice-locked seas. For 10 days in October, Eskimos, environmentalists, oil company workers, U.S. government officials, scientists and Soviet seamen carved the rescue by the sheer force of human determination. As Roger Rosenblatt observed on the PBS television network's *MacNeil Lehrer News Hour*, "While two whales are deliberately saved, others are deliberately killed." But might not one hopefully ask, "As the conscience of conservation shifts from the dim memories of yesterday to the uncertainties of tomorrow, cannot we hold in our hearts the shining hour of today?"

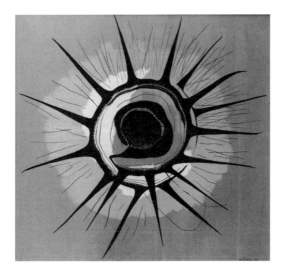

ACKNOWLEDGMENTS

THIS VOLUME ARISES FROM MY WRITTEN AND SPOKEN WORDS of the last 40 years, not to mention the sounds of marine life and bird calls and even the husky cry of a cougar. But it was Beulah Trist who volunteered to gather many of my papers and print them in large type to clarify my memories. I also drew on notes from my oral history, *Artist, and Wildlife and Environmental Defender*, recorded and gathered from 1986 to 88 by Suzanne Reiss and Ann Lage, and published by the Regents of the University of California, Berkeley in 1991. My writings for the Friends of the Sea Otter appear here as well, from the publication, *The Otter Raft*, including the first page written in 1960 in a column that later became known as "Cliffside Seat."

I am deeply indebted to Dr. James Mattison, Jr., the first underwater photographer of sea otters, and the first individual to feature their underwater habitat in a film. And to Bobbie Harms, who ran our first sea otter center for nine years, and kept me steady as well. For her scientific wisdom and her leadership, all who knew her thank the late Dr. Betty Davis. And Carol Fulton, whose quick mind kept us all laughing, even in times of stress. Our thanks to Jud Vandervere, who served as our naturalist and teacher.

It is with deep gratitude that I remember the late senator Fred Farr, who worked with me to remove the bounty on the mountain lion; and Wallace Stegner who wrote those golden words about the cougar—"your passing could prick the stillness and bring everything to the alert."

My earliest influences were from my father, Frank W. Wentworth, who worked closely with Newton Drury, founder of the Save-the-Redwoods League, serving as chair of the finance committee and working assiduously to start the Memorial Groves in 1930. My father was succeeded by his son, William Wentworth, who served as treasurer for 25 years. In the past year, my nephew, Frank Wentworth, took over as treasurer and director.

But it was Nora Deans, publisher at the Monterey Bay Aquarium, who tastefully took the material for this small volume and pressed her devotion on each segment to make it a whole, with the detailed assistance of Roxane Buck-Ezcurra and Christina Joie Slager, and the design of Carole Thickstun. And with great respect, I thank Julie Packard, who reaches with hope for the message that we have not lost our connection with nature, and the sea along our shores.

Awards, Honors and Achievements

AWARDS
Lifetime Achievement Award
Children's Health Environmental Coalition, 1996

Distinguished Service Award
Sierra Club, 1991

Conservation Award
Daughters of the American Revolution, 1990

Gold Medal
United Nations Environment Program, 1988

A. Starker Leopole Award
California Nature Conservancy, 1986

The Audubon Medal for Distinguished Service to Conservation
National Audubon Society, 1983

The Joseph Wood Krutch Award for significant contribution toward the
improvement of life and the environment
The Humane Society of the United States, 1980

Conservation Award
American Motors, 1980

Conservation Award
California Academy of Sciences, 1979

Gold Medal, Conservation Service Award
United States Department of the Interior, 1975

HONORS
Honorary Member
California State Park Rangers Association, 1998

Honorary Doctorate
Mills College

Honorary Board Member
Sierra Club

ACHIEVEMENTS
Commissioner, California State Parks, 1963-69

Member, National Parks Foundation Board, 1968-69

Member, Board of Directors, African Wildlife Leadership Foundation, 1968-80

Member, Board of Trustees, Defenders of Wildlife, 1969-74

Founder/President, Friends of the Sea Otter, 1969-90

Chair, California Mountain Lion Preservation Foundation, 1987

Trustee, Environmental Defense Fund, 1972-83

Regional Trustee, Mills College, 1962-68